Better Boards, Better Schools

The ISM Guide for Private School Trusteeship and Strategic Governance

Better Boards, Better Schools
The ISM Guide to Private School Trusteeship and Strategic Governance

Independent School Management, Inc.
1316 N. Union Street, Wilmington, DE 19806

All rights reserved. No part of this book may be reproduced or transmitted in any form or by any means, electronic or mechanical, including photocopying, scanning, recording, or by any information storage and retrieval system without the permission of Independent School Management, except for use within the school only.

Disclaimer: Independent School Management provides management consulting and other services to private schools. ISM is not a law firm. No service or information provided by ISM should be construed as legal advice. All references in this book are correct as of the publication date, but may have become inactive or otherwise modified since that time.

Copyright © 2019 by Independent School Management, Inc.

Printed in the United States of America

ISBN-13: 978-1-883627-21-8

Contents

Introduction 5

CHAPTER ONE
The Role of the Trustee 7

CHAPTER TWO
The Board's Foundation and Strategic Structures 15

CHAPTER THREE
Understanding Private School Finances 39

CHAPTER FOUR
Strategic Planning and Strategic Financial Planning 51

CHAPTER FIVE
The ISM Stability Markers 95

CHAPTER SIX
Purpose and Outcome Statements 111

CHAPTER SEVEN
ISM Success Predictors 119

CHAPTER EIGHT
Recruiting and Orienting Board Members 127

CHAPTER NINE
The Board Committees 143

CHAPTER TEN
Board Meetings and Other Functions 171

CHAPTER ELEVEN
Board-School Head Relationships 187

CHAPTER TWELVE
The Board's Role in Fundraising 201

CHAPTER THIRTEEN
Strategic Board Assessment 213

CHAPTER FOURTEEN
A Sample Board Commitment and Trustee Handbook 221

APPENDICES
The Student Experience Profile 231

The Faculty Culture Profile 239

The ISM Executive Leadership Study 247

Faculty Experience Survey 253

Introduction

Independent School Management (ISM) is a family-owned company dedicated to the advancement of private school management. ISM reaches over 7,000 private-independent schools and serves over 200,000 students annually with advice, assistance, and creative solutions. Administrators in private schools of all types and sizes turn to ISM as they deal with an array of management challenges, including student recruitment and retention, fundraising, strategic and long-range planning, Board-Head relations, personnel, plant expansion, mergers, leadership training, and creative insurance solutions.

This book is based on more than four decades of working with the Boards of hundreds of private schools. We've honed our research and recommendations over those years to provide the best possible service to our schools. We hope you'll find the following theory and advice valuable as you prepare your Board to plan for your school's future.

Throughout this book, we use a fictional, K–12, coed day school, Exempli Gratia Academy, to provide examples and samples to better explain the strategies and techniques discussed. These examples are intentionally generic in nature so that you can easily adapt them for your school's unique character and mission.

CHAPTER ONE

The Role of the Trustee

Serving as a member of the Board of Trustees for a private school is certainly an honor. You are being asked to take into your care a school—the entire student body. You must ensure that each student's education fulfills the school's mission, and that all students are nurtured and developed to their benefit. You are going to carry out that care by providing support—resources—to the School Head, the Board's sole employee who carries out the Board's decisions. Your relationship to the school determines your school's success in the long term.

Being a Board member is also somewhat puzzling. If you're like many Trustees, you're not sure how it happened. Maybe you were approached at a social event. Maybe another Board member had talked to you about it on the phone; you may even have forgotten the conversation. Maybe you were serving on a committee and this seemed the next logical step.

It's also most likely that you are the parent of a student at the school. This makes being a Trustee more complicated. After all, surely you have a right to advocate for your child, right? Being a Board member gives you rather more opportunity to do that. Other parents, in fact, talk to you about their issues as well, hoping that you can help influence the process. In Board discussions, you imagine the impact of your decisions on your children and on your family, particularly when it comes to setting tuition.

Whatever your circumstances, the following two considerations are key as we begin this exploration of what you do as a Trustee.

1. You are a volunteer. This means:

   - This is not the only thing you do! Being a Trustee is no higher than four or five of your other top priorities (less important than, for example, being a family person, having a career, being involved with your religious institution, and so on).
   - The Board meets infrequently—maybe 10 meetings a year of an average two hours' duration, i.e., about 20 hours annually. Now, this obviously doesn't include other responsibilities such as serving on a committee, attending events, and engaging in fundraising activities. But the decision-making function the Board exercises is carried out within a small band of time.

2. You believe in the mission of the school. If you are a parent, you have seen the power of the school's mission in the lives of your children. You have firsthand experience of the faculty's commitment and have at least an inkling of the challenges faced by the School Head and Leadership Team. If you are not a parent, you have a picture of what this school can do for children in the community in which you live, for society as a whole. You agree with the mission and, without being myopic, you support the school unconditionally. You may know parents at the school and vicariously enjoy their children's successes.

These key considerations—being a volunteer and believing in the mission—have enormous ramifications. Whatever other roles you may play as a parent, committee member, donor and so on, your role as Trustee is fundamentally carried out in two ways. As a Trustee, you:

– support the mission, and

– act strategically (from the perspective of a grandparent) to ensure the school is there for the next generation.

You don't have time to do anything else.

Nine Characteristics of the Responsible Trustee

As you ponder your role as a Board member, consider the following nine-item "Responsible Trustee" list—a general set of "due diligence" behaviors and attitudes. The list is not prioritized.

1. **The Responsible Trustee comes to Board meetings well-prepared and on time, is attentive to the business at hand, and stays for all of every meeting.** Each Trustee is expected to review the "homework" assigned, whether specific to the committee on which she or he serves, or general and applicable to the entire Board (such as the School Head's report).

2. **The Responsible Trustee has respect for the confidentiality of each Board meeting.** Each Trustee should understand that communication from Board to constituents is the responsibility of the authorized Board spokesperson(s). Board-level information that is not released—or has not yet been released—through an "official" communications vehicle should be considered absolutely confidential. The "leaking" of information from Board-level discussions is damaging and may be catastrophic. Public discussion of in-process issues feeds your local grapevine, which then swells with incomplete and distorted information about Board perspectives and decisions.

3. **The Responsible Trustee insists on seeing the (potential) long-range consequences of all decisions.** Boards exist to make viability-focused decisions for coming generations of families and their children. This perspective (which may be readily written into a Board-level mission statement for your governing body) transmits all deliberations to their proper longer-term context. Even apparently short-term decisions (e.g., which audit firm to hire this year) may have long-term consequences. Adopting this perspective tends to drive policy creation, so short-term decisions are taken in the context of a policy framework that will remain in place to guide related decisions.

4. **The Responsible Trustee asks for data, both hard (quantitative) and soft (qualitative).** Each Trustee should learn to ask for evidence bearing on any issue under consideration. Boardroom statements that begin with phrases such as, "I hear that ..." or "More and more kids are ..." or "Parents are up in arms about ..." should be challenged by requests for evidence and, without such, set aside. An appropriate next step would be to suggest collecting pertinent data, coupled with postponing further discussion until

the next meeting.

5. **The Responsible Trustee persists in asking about the appropriate level of Board activity.** A critical annual procedural step comes in the summer when the Board leadership and the School Head establish the annual Board agenda and the annual operations agenda. Both agendas are derived largely from items in the upcoming year's strategic plan and strategic financial plan. Close monitoring of progress on these parallel agendas, by the Chairs of the Committee on Trustees and the Head Support and Evaluation Committee, turns this question—proper Board activity level—into a readily answerable one. (We will discuss the annual agendas and Board committees in later chapters.) Bear in mind, however, there is a gray area here that may imply one level of Board activity in one context and a different level of Board activity in another. For example, the Board activity in a small school that functions without a full-time Development Director differs from a large school that has a staff of five.

6. **The Responsible Trustee maintains an awareness that the School Head does not report to individual Board members, but to the Board as the institution's governing body.** If the Committee on Trustees Chair finds that any Trustee conducts herself or himself in such a way to imply something contrary to this basic principle, that Trustee must be re-educated immediately. In the face of persistent violation of this principle, the Board removes the person.

7. **The Responsible Trustee who has children in the school must carefully distinguish between parental perspective and responsibility, on the one hand, and Trusteeship perspective and responsibility, on the other.** No Trustee may wear the "parent hat" at Board meetings, since Trustees' fundamental responsibilities are to generations yet unborn. (See the reference in No. 3, above, to a Board-level mission statement that focuses the Board's attention on future generations of families and their children.)

8. **The Responsible Trustee is the champion of all the school's fundraising efforts.** Each Trustee must understand that leadership in all fundraising efforts is fundamental to her or his commitment as a Board member. Taking the lead means giving generously within each individual's capacity to annual, capital, endowment, and major gifts initiatives. The message from the Board leadership is clear: "As Trustees, we see the school as one of our top philanthropic activities. We donate to every campaign and give to the fullest extent of our capabilities." When donors and

prospects know that 100% of your Board gives philanthropically, they are inspired to give.

9. **The Responsible Trustee gives unqualified public support to the School Head, the administration, the faculty, and her or his colleagues.** Each Trustee must understand the time and place to disagree is in Board meetings, not in public. Public criticism of teachers, administrators, or other Trustees is devastating to the school culture and to the Board and Head's leadership. As with other areas of Board interactions with constituents, Board-level policies can help immensely, offering points of reference (e.g., "Our Board's policy is not to comment on … but instead, to encourage you to …").

The Trustee as Parent

You're on the playground and a parent comes up to you and says, "What do you think of the way the Board has dealt with the dress code?" What do you say? As a parent you may want to say, "Oh, that's terrible. I can't imagine what's got into them!" But you've just been elected to the Board of Trustees. What response should you make?

As part of your orientation, you've almost certainly been given some documents, introduced to the Board President, and thanked by the School Head. You may even have attended a retreat where you talked about the next strategic planning and strategic financial planning cycle. Hopefully, you've also received advice on how to handle your parent role. The main points might have looked something like this:

Although you still think of yourself as a parent, once everyone else knows that you are a Board member, no one will think of you as just a parent! Every statement you make will be treated as if it is a Board opinion. The gossip that "he or she said" will now have more weight given to it. Those dissatisfied with the direction the Board is taking will use your opinion to back them up, as will those who are supportive. Solutions that you should consider include:

– only attending functions where there are groups of people, i.e., not getting into one-on-one conversations;

– keeping to topics that do not involve Board policy or personality;

– politely deferring school-related topics to the School Head or other appropriate school official; and

– providing a concise summary of the Board's decision and reasons for acting.

As a Trustee, you will be scrutinized carefully about your opinion of the School Head. It will be difficult at times, but it is critical that your public assessment of the Head's performance be relentlessly upbeat. Your support of the school and its personnel is a litmus test for other parents of the confidence they have in the school's future. Whatever your private feelings, and however you express your thoughts within the Board meetings, your support of the Head in public is unwavering. Only the Board as a whole can change its opinion. Think of a phrase that will help you get away from such discussions. Depending on the situation, the following might be helpful.

- The Board fully supports the School Head.
- I do not comment on the School Head's performance.
- I really appreciate the School Head's leadership.
- That's a question our School Head would be able to answer much better than I could.
- I'm a Board member—we deal with the strategic role. This is an operations question and you would have to ask the Head about that.

You must recognize that you now have power in a way that, as a parent, you didn't. You are part of a group that has the ability to close the school, hire or fire the Head, make financial decisions that can affect the careers of individuals, revise and change the mission statement. Whether you "feel" it or not, your power makes you much more difficult to deal with. Have some sympathy for teachers who appear a little less certain in their interactions with you. Recognize (and appreciate) the care with which administrators couch their conversations with you. Never use your position to exert influence in operational school affairs.

You need to be able to advocate effectively for your child. When you approach an administrator or teacher, make the person as comfortable as possible by saying something like: "I want to talk with you about Isaac's progress in mathematics. I'm here as Isaac's parent, not in my role as Board member. I want you to know that our conversation will stay between you and our family." Some Trustees find it helpful to have their spouse or partner make advocacy approaches.

Your new role as a Trustee is an important one to the future of the school. Keep a sense of proportion—you, as an individual, still don't have any real power. The Board operates as an entity and each individual exerts power only as a part of the whole. Stay humble. Keep a sense of humor. Whether you are on the Board for a couple of years or a decade, it won't be forever. And your family is still your more important priority. Laugh at yourself a little. Keep a sense of service. It's not about power anyway. You know that. You joined the Board to be able to serve the school with your wealth, your wisdom, your energy. You (should) have no interest in and no part in power politics. Enjoy the opportunity to exercise servant leadership and ensure that, at the end, there's nothing that you regret, and the school is stronger because of the service you provided.

CHAPTER TWO

The Board's Foundation and Strategic Structures

Your School's Charter

A school becomes a legal entity when its charter is accepted by the appropriate government agency for filing. This fundamental document, also known—depending on the state—as a Certificate of Incorporation or Articles of Incorporation, sets forth the corporation's purpose. Traditionally, this document defines, limits, and regulates the powers of the school, its Board of Trustees, and its officers.

Keep It Simple

When the Board begins a charter review, keep in mind that a charter should be a simple, enabling document. Provide the broadest possible framework, one that leaves options open and accommodates changes that might occur down the road. Avoid references to specific grade levels, single-sex or coed status, and educational style.

The institution's leaders should be free to respond to needs as they determine them and to operate with efficiency. They should not be limited by a narrow document. Avoid ambiguous terms so the school's own charter cannot be used against it in a court case, should an individual or group desire to prove the school operates in a manner not legally authorized.

Some of the information that was once required in a charter may now be unnecessary, depending on the circumstances in the state within which the school was and is incorporated. Some states have established routine corporate powers by statute: powers such as purchasing, investing, leasing, building, and borrowing. If you find that these are not included by your state's legislation, then they will need to be listed in your charter. Other states have established specific not-for-profit law at the state level designed to apply specifically to schools, colleges, and other such entities.

Some states permit sections relating to the Board of Trustees and officers covered in bylaws rather than charters. In fact, *details of organization and operation should be covered in the bylaws, not the charter, whenever possible. As such, they are readily changed, requiring only Board action without directly involving your state bureaucracy.*

School charters tend to be much alike, except in the sections that deal with liquidation of assets, and possibly, qualifications of Board members. These areas need periodic review because relationships and purposes change.

For example, some schools established with a religious affiliation have, over the years, reduced or dissolved those ties. In such instances, it may no longer be appropriate for a school's assets to be turned over to the affiliated group should the school cease to operate, but the original charter may still require this action. Also, a school may find the incorporation document calls for a majority of the Board members to be associated with the original religious organization, a position the school has moved away from over the years.

Updating the Charter

A charter should not be cast in stone. Like a will, update it from time to time to reflect change and current circumstances. Procedures exist in each jurisdiction for making alterations.

A well-written charter can help resolve problems. For example, the Internal Revenue Service has, occasionally, interpreted activities such as camping, swimming, and even reading to be "unrelated business," and taxable.

Imagine now that Exempli Gratia Academy, ISM's fictional K–12 day school, finds itself in the following situation. When the (hypothetical) school was founded in 1902, its charter established the institution's right to conduct programs of academic, moral, and physical education. The founders could not have envisioned the large, community-oriented, multiprogrammed entity the school has become. In particular, they could not have anticipated the summer programs that make use of the campus and the faculty.

Imagine, as well, that the IRS takes the position that Exempli Gratia Academy's summer programs comprise "unrelated business," and proposes to tax those components of the school's operations. This (imaginary) skirmish over interpretation of taxable activities prompts the school to petition its state bureaucracy for the following changes in its charter.

> ***Exempli Gratia Academy is chartered (in addition to other stipulations and authorizations in this document) to offer to students, including students involved during its regular terms, summer programs of academic, supplemental training, and tutoring; music education and training in the arts; physical education; driver education; training in computers, sports, citizenship, safety, and health education; and other educational services to members of the communities which it serves.***

> ***Exempli Gratia Academy is chartered (in addition to other stipulations and authorizations in this document) to offer credit and noncredit courses to adults in academic subjects, including but not limited to English, history, science, mathematics, language, the arts, music, computers, physical education, and recreational sports. These courses and programs may be offered on evenings, weekends, and during the summer.***

Responses to petitions to government agencies may take months or even years to process. The Committee on Trustees should be proactive in conducting a charter review as a matter of routine and regular due diligence. To make doubly sure that this due diligence comes to the Board's attention on a scheduled basis, consider placing "charter review" in each new iteration of your strategic planning document. Making this—strategic planning—a quadrennial Board of Trustees activity, then this due diligence becomes part of your Board's regular strategic-plan-related activities.

Your Board's Mission

Now that you understand the true function of the strategic Board, it's time to talk about mission.

Can your school's Trustees define their job in 30 words or less? That's the goal in developing a Board mission statement—a concise reason-for-being against which the organization's members can measure their agenda items, discussions, and decisions.

On the one hand, Trustees support the school's mission as a part of their "trust." On the other hand, this can lead you to believe that, to fulfill your role as a Trustee, you must know what's going on in the school—in each classroom, in the curriculum, and with each teacher. You may feel the School Head should be giving a report at every Board meeting about the state of the school, and that you should be fundamentally concerned with these matters. Nothing is further from the truth!

Consider this scenario: A Trustee questions the competency of a fourth-grade teacher. The Board decides its involvement is warranted. A committee is created to review curriculum, oversee the Head's teacher evaluations, survey parents to get their opinions of the faculty, and direct the Head to replace any teachers the committee determines are "questionable."

Dramatic? Situations like this play out in schools across the country, year after year. Boards have various beliefs about the appropriate boundaries for their actions. These boundaries can fluctuate, depending on the Board's leadership for any given year, the experience and strength of the Head, and the quality of the relationship between the Board President and the Head.

The Board hired the School Head to handle those operational matters. Support the School Head through your strategic role and exercise your own due diligence. To make sure you properly understand your relationship to the school mission, ensure that your Board has its own mission statement.

In ISM's experience, most Boards have not taken this step. Sometimes it's because they didn't think of it. Other times, it's because mission seems like a vague concept with little practical application. In other cases, it's because the individual Trustees could not agree on the Board's fundamental mission. If you don't have a Board mission statement, develop one with the following thoughts in mind. If you do have one, review it based on these principles.

- The Board is to support the school's mission, not in the sense of opposing all change, but in the sense of being true to it and being intentional about any changes.

- The mission is always central to the decision-making process. How does a plan of action support or not support the mission?

- The mission must continue to develop. Revisit the mission statement every eight years (that's every second strategic plan and strategic financial plan). Also reconsider the mission whenever major changes or events occur—a building project is completed, the student population increases or decreases dramatically, the program changes, or the school goes through an accreditation process.

- The Board must take viability-related action. This bluntly means that you must ensure the school (Leadership Team) has the resources needed to carry out the mission in the life of its students. This typically includes funding, facilities, support for programs, the hiring of enough administrators, public affirmation of the school, and so on.

- Financially, the Board's important roles include setting tuition, donating money, soliciting donations from others, renewing and building facilities, and setting the budget.

The Board takes such actions to benefit not the current students but the children of the current students, with the following implications.

- It is conceivable the results of the actions taken will not be fully (or even largely) realized in the time you are on the Board. Examples might include the attempt to improve faculty compensation over time (with a 10-year time line), or the desire to build endowment (with a 50-year time line).

- It is conceivable the Board will allow a current dilemma to go unresolved because it is part of a broader issue. For example, the lack of air-conditioning in a classroom may continue as you develop a Campus Master Development Plan enabling the Board to address the situation in a far more permanent and effective fashion.

- It is also conceivable the Board will take direct action to solve a "now" problem because it is also a future problem. For example, you might support the faculty (at the School Head's request) by increasing the academic budget line to renew each curricular area in turn on a rotational basis.

- The power of the Board's mission statement is that the conversation is always brought back to the basic question: What are you here for? The mission statement answers that question: We're here to support the school mission, ensuring that our actions are always student-centered and ensure viability to the next generation.

Writing the Mission Statement

As the Board plans the annual retreat, set aside a two-hour session dedicated to creating the Board mission statement. Your statement should:

- be no more than 30 words long;
- be value-laden;
- clearly identify the Board's focus;
- be specific (rather than comprehensive); and
- identify the difference-makers.

Before the retreat, send each Trustee a short list of the roles that effective Boards fulfill. Under each one, list the actions the Board has undertaken to support those roles.

A sample might look like this.

Preserve the school's mission
- February 2019: Review of the school's mission statement
- October 2019: Approval of a Development Gift Policy aligned with the school's mission

Strategic planning and strategic financial planning
- April 2019: Strategic planning session carried out
- Reviewed April 2018 and 2019

Sustain the strategic factors that support the faculty culture
- April 2019: Strategic item to increase professional development funds by $5,000 each year of the strategic plan

Major gift cultivation
- September 2018: Committee on Trustees charged with identifying two potential Trustees who are bonded to the school and wealthy enough to make a major gift

For the discussion, identify items the Board has dealt with that are not included on this list because they were not strategic (governance-focused) but operational (management-focused). Consider the difference between those two types of items. Reinforce that the Board's focus should be on its strategic role.

The Board should have the greatest confidence that the School Head, its only employee, will carry out the operational items.

Finally, take ISM's generic Board mission statement below and use it as a template in creating your own.

> ***The Exempli Gratia Academy Board of Trustees is committed to supporting the mission of the school by taking viability-focused action for the next generation of students.***

Note that this process is directive, not an open-ended discussion. There is a right answer. The Board's roles are few but critical, directed toward ensuring that the school remains viable and vital so that it can continue to educate children and serve families. Counsel off Board members who disagree substantially with these positions and want to take charge of day-to-day operations.

With the mission statement in place, the Board has a means for maintaining its focus, even through leadership changes. The statement also provides the Committee on Trustees with an important parameter to use in seeking, finding, and recruiting appropriate Board members.

Strategic Board Bylaws

While there is no standard approach to drafting private school bylaws, Boards should periodically review these items to:

- make them clearer, simpler, and more utilitarian; and
- bring them more fully into the day-to-day life of the Board and of the school.

Your Board exists to ensure the institution's mission is viable for the current students' yet-to-be-born children—the primary constituency it serves. An orientation toward the future is implicit. Thus, it follows that strategic planning and strategic financial planning is any Board's core activity—i.e., creating and overseeing the implementation of a viability-focused institutional road map.

Implications for Bylaws

Consider revisiting your Board's bylaws to determine the extent to which they reflect and promote that core planning activity. If they do, or if your Board's leadership is willing to edit or rewrite them so they will, then your bylaws can become an integral component in your Board's structure and function. The following outline may be helpful as you review your bylaws to ascertain the extent to which they are "strategic." Recommended ingredients in such an approach include the following.

An approval (cover) sheet. A cover sheet showing your bylaws' date of approval, with appropriate signature(s), and with ratifications, if any, from other authorities (e.g., a parent religious body) provides a suitable introductory page.

A philosophical source sheet. Consider quotations from relevant sources (e.g., Aristotle, Plato, Horace, and other philosophers; in religiously affiliated school settings, from a Holy Scripture; in Montessori school settings, from Dr. Maria Montessori). These serve to remind readers that a meaningful set of bylaws is designed to promote a particular educational or spiritual belief consistent with your school's mission.

Several pages displaying: (a) the institutional mission statement and (b) the current strategic plan. Limit your mission statement to 30 words and your strategic plan to two or three pages. If your mission and strategic plan are of those lengths, they can be easily displayed in your bylaw document. If they are longer, then provide summaries. Next, begin linking your bylaws with your mission and plan strategically, distinct from a mere summarization of your institution's legal underpinnings. Having become strategic, bylaws then become relevant in a new way, helping Board leaders to fit structure and function to mission and plan.

Definitions. A page that defines terms (e.g., Board, bylaws, School Head, school, and other words and phrases used repeatedly in the document) provides an obvious opportunity to couch your bylaws in "strategic" terms. For example, "Board" may be defined as "the self-perpetuating entity charged with the strategic, longest-term protection and strengthening of the financial, physical, and programmatic assets of the institution." "Head" may be defined as "the institution's Chief Executive Officer and the Board's only employee." These definitions help to frame the Board's responsibilities strategically and in relationship to the school and to its Head.

Purposes and Powers. A page devoted to statements of purposes and powers can introduce the aforementioned "legal underpinnings" without diluting the strategic and philosophical thrust of the bylaws. For example, you may add the following statement. "The school is organized exclusively for educational purposes within the context of Section 501(c)(3) of the United States Internal Revenue Service Code, or the corresponding provision of any future law of this nation." The school's "educational purposes" are those expressed in its institutional mission statement.

Board of Trustees (Directors, Governors, etc.). This heading introduces the self-descriptive (structure and function) components of the detailed bylaws listing, and displays several subheads, such as the following.

Board-Specific Stipulations

Powers. As the opening subhead under "Board of Trustees," this section should define the Board's legal and organizational capabilities more specifically than in the previous "purposes and powers" section. The language should reflect the centrality of the Board's strategic planning and strategic financial planning responsibilities. The following language is illustrative.

All the affairs and business of the school will be managed by the Board in a manner consistent with these bylaws and other applicable state and local constraints. The Board focuses on:

- strategic planning and strategic financial planning, and the annual agendas derived from the resulting planning document(s);
- policy setting and policy implementation consistent with and pursuant to the planning document(s);
- employment and evaluation of a School Head who functions as the Chief Executive Officer, on the Board's behalf, of the operations-level implementation of the planning document's component parts.

The Board makes appropriate delegations of authority to the Board President and to the School Head. To the extent permitted by law, the Board may authorize, by appropriate resolution, one or more Board committees to act on its behalf when it is not in session.

Besides the general powers conferred by these bylaws, the specific powers of the Board include, without limitation, the power to:

- elect a President from the Board members;
- receive and hold by purchase, gift, etc., real or personal property for educational purposes connected with or for the benefit of the school;
- develop and revise as needed both an overall strategic plan and a corresponding strategic financial plan, to develop revenue sources and to establish expenditure systems consistent with those plans;
- approve an annual budget consistent with the strategic financial plan;
- determine the compensation package for the School Head;
- having hired the School Head, either extend the Head's contract in a systematic and timely manner or, in likewise manner, bring it to closure;

- grant and confer diplomas (via the School Head and the faculty) to those completing the school's courses of study; and
- amend these bylaws as necessary.

Number and Election of Trustees. The language of your bylaws—here and elsewhere—must be permissive, not prescriptive. Rather than, for example, specifying the number of Board members required, the bylaw should provide either a maximum number (e.g., no more than 22 members) or a range (e.g., 17 to 22 members). This approach allows the Board to make a strategic determination about the ideal number of Trustees needed to carry out the planning document's implications at a given juncture.

This approach also allows the Board to avoid being forced by its own bylaws to fill seats with less-than-ideal new members. The following language is illustrative.

The Board of Trustees consists of not less than 17 or more than 22 members. Following the recommendations of new members by the Committee on Trustees, all Trustees are elected by the existing Board of Trustees by simple majority vote.

The guiding principle for the Committee on Trustees' recommendations, and for the full Board's subsequent approval, will be each (potential) new Trustee's willingness and capacity to further the school's mission and its currently approved strategic plan.

Thus, selecting new Trustees for your Board becomes part of the strategic school development process and is grounded in the language of the bylaw document itself.

Tenure of Trustees. Establish three-year terms that can be renewed once, followed by at least one (mandatory) year off the Board. However, "strategic" bylaws should include the stipulation that a Trustee appointment to a particular strategically focused responsibility be allowed to override this general (three-years-times-two) constraint. For example, if a member is elected as Board President at the start of her or his sixth year, then extend that six-year term to coincide with the normal term served by Board Presidents in your school.

Meetings, Notice, Quorum, etc. Boards should not stipulate in the bylaws a specific frequency of meetings, but simply state a minimum number of annual meetings (e.g., three) and include language to this effect.

The Board President will annually—normally during early summer—establish and publish the upcoming year's calendar of Board meetings as a function of the strategic plan's implications for the annual Board agenda. The primary rationale for establishing Board meeting dates will be the expected schedule of Board committee proposals to be discussed and voted on. The primary rationale for committee proposal development is furthering the strategic plan. Thus, the Board meeting calendar will be designed annually in such a manner as to advance the strategic plan in the most efficient way possible.

Manner of Acting, Resignations and Removal, Proxies, Vacancies, Compensation, Procedure, Advisory Board, Conflict of Interest. (The manner of acting may be formal or informal; proxies and compensation are prohibited.) Strategic bylaws differ little, if at all, from traditional bylaws in subsections such as these. If there is a perceptible difference, it is in the brevity and simplicity of strategic bylaws. They are designed to communicate, in the most user-friendly fashion possible, the basic strategic framework for Board structure and function. For example, one-sentence paragraphs such as "Proxies are not allowed" or "No Trustee will receive compensation for Board service" are sufficient and complete as written.

Committees. "Strategic" bylaws emphasize the primacy of strategic process over the concept of standing committees. The following language illustrates this point:

Committee structure and function are determined annually by a process that begins with the Board President re-examination of the strategic plan (see previous Section on "Meetings, Notice, Quorum, etc."). This review, normally conducted each summer, results in creating the annual Board agenda—the schedule of actions for the upcoming year. This is followed by the determination of the exact committee structure most appropriate for fulfilling that agenda.

The Board President selects committee Chairs and, in consultation with the Chairs, develops lists of Trustees and non-Trustees to fill the roles in each committee with the individuals best suited to advance that committee's charge—and the overall strategic plan—during the year.

Although this strategic approach mitigates against standing committees, four committees are likely to be renewed annually regardless of the exact Board agenda that is developed: Committee on Trustees, Head Support and Evaluation Committee, Finance Committee, and Development Committee with its subcommittees Annual Fund and Major Gifts.

The President appoints committees as needed to implement the strategic plan.

Officers. In a strategic approach to Board structure and function, the conventional array of officers often becomes a bureaucratic anachronism.

A President is needed, certainly. Any responsibilities a Treasurer would handle can be reasonably discharged by the Chair of the Finance Committee. A skilled clerical person, preferably the Administrative Assistant of a Trustee, takes the minutes. The clerical person would be paid for his or her services by the Trustee, as a gift-in-kind to the institution. The following strategic bylaw language is illustrative.

> *The Board shall elect a President to serve a term the length of which shall be recommended by the Committee on Trustees. That committee examines the strategic plan and the (prospective or newly elected) President's qualifications to lead the Board through the plan's various stages.*
>
> *The Board Treasurer's functions, if any, shall be discharged by the Chair of the Finance Committee.*
>
> *Board minutes shall be recorded, transcribed, and circulated by a qualified clerical person hired to perform these duties with great discretion. That individual shall not be a Trustee or employed by the school or related by marriage or birth to any employee of the school.*
>
> *In the President's absence, the Chair of the Finance Committee shall preside.*

Duties of the President. The President's duties, besides the obvious one of presiding at Board meetings, are summarized in the foregoing section titled "Committees."

Duties of the School Head. While the Head's role has been defined briefly elsewhere in this document, a separate section may be useful. The following language is illustrative.

> *The School Head, the Board's only employee, will be the Chief Executive Officer of all school operations. Subject to the ultimate authority of the Board, the School Head supervises and controls all the business and affairs of the institution with no Board-level interference. (Board involvement in operations may be explicitly requested by the Head to assist in a particular exigency.)*
>
> *The Head, in particular, advances the institution's Board-approved strategic plan and that plan's financial subset, the strategic financial plan, at the operations level. The Head is held accountable for doing so by the Head*

Support and Evaluation Committee of the Board.

The Head, although not a member of the Board, presents at all full-Board meetings save any during which the Head's performance or compensation is under review. (The Head may be invited to be present during such review.)

The Head's role within the Board committee structure (aside from Head Support and Evaluation Committee meetings, at which the Head will always be present) is dictated by the implications of the annual Board and operations agendas. However, the Head's presence at meetings of the Committee on Trustees and sub-committees of the Development Committee will normally be "strategic," regardless of the details of the two agendas in a given year.

Contracts, Gifts, Fiscal Year Defined, Indemnification, Amendments. These subsections will be displayed in "strategic" bylaws just as they are in conventional approaches to bylaw construction. Regardless of a Board's strategic orientation (or not), bylaws need paragraphs authorizing the Board's and the institution's entry into contractual agreements, approving the receipt of gifts (monetary and other), specifying the institution's fiscal year, indemnifying the Board and its members in all good-faith actions and transactions, and specifying the process of amending the bylaws.

Committee Summaries in Bylaws. As you develop or reconsider your bylaws, your Board committees should be well-defined. The following wording is illustrative.

Summarize the core structure and function of the four strategic committees.

Committee on Trustees. Form a Committee on Trustees for the purposes and activities listed as following.

- The Committee on Trustees periodically reviews the strategic plan to ascertain the Board's personnel needs—professional mix, financial mix, and other—in upcoming years.
- The Committee on Trustees then profiles the Board, listing the ideal characteristics implicit in the most appropriate mix of members needed for fulfilling the strategic plan's goals. This mix may include expertise in finance, land development, nonprofit marketing, nonprofit management, plant maintenance, and access to various wealth networks.
- The Committee on Trustees then identifies individuals whose characteristics and backgrounds (cumulatively) fulfill the profile.

- The Committee on Trustees then formulates a cultivation plan to bring those individuals to eventual Board (and Board committee) membership.
- The Committee on Trustees oversees the cultivation process.
- The Committee on Trustees nominates cultivated individuals for Board and Board committee membership.
- The Committee on Trustees devises and implements one or more annual Board orientation sessions for the newly elected members.
- The Committee on Trustees conducts an evaluation of the Board on (at least) an annual basis. This evaluation is based on the level of excellence with which the Board has met its annual Board agenda. The evaluation focuses on the Board's overall success, but will include individuals and individual committees (including the Board President), as needed and as appropriate. The objective of the evaluation is the ongoing strengthening of the Board.

Since the Committee on Trustees "balances the power" within the Board's internal structure, its Chair and composition will not be determined by the Board President, but by whole-Board election. (The Committee on Trustees may choose to recommend to the whole Board its own successors in the same way that it may choose to recommend to the President other committee leadership and membership positions.)

Head Support and Evaluation Committee. The Board President may appoint the Head Support and Evaluation Committee (HSEC) to discharge the Board's responsibility to ensure the strategic plan's advancement at the operations level.

The HSEC works in concert with the School Head to delineate several annual major objectives, each of which clearly advances the strategic plan or corrects an operations-level weakness or problem.

The HSEC comprises no more than five members, a minority of whom may be requested by the School Head, and all of whom qualify as capable mentors and advisors for the Head. A minority may be non-Board members.

Finance Committee. The Board President may appoint a Finance Committee to develop the details of a strategic financial plan (a subset of the overall strategic plan). The committee develops and recommends to the full Board an annual operations budget that conforms to, and efficiently advances, the strategic plan and its financial components. The Chair of the Finance Committee acts as Board Treasurer when that function is required.

Development Committee. The Board President may appoint a Development Committee to develop the details of an overall external affairs and institutional advancement framework consistent with, and in furtherance of, the strategic plan. As circumstances warrant, the annual fund and major gifts programs may be organized under separate subcommittees, reporting to the Development Committee. (See Chapter Nine.)

Board Bylaws, Institutional Dissolution, and Bylaw Changes

One aspect of the due diligence rightly expected of the Board President is a periodic review of Board bylaws. Review them at least quadrennially, for accuracy, relevance, and technical legal compliance with appropriate statutes. If you also aspire to implement ISM's strategic Board concepts, have the bylaws altered to reflect those aspirations.

A section of school bylaws that is frequently omitted or carelessly done is the section on dissolution. If included at all, it often comprises the final paragraph(s) of the bylaw document. The dissolution section is your institution's official, legally endorsed (by federal, state, and local statutes) statement of the desired and appropriate disposition of school assets in the event of school closure—for any reason, at any point in the future. Whether your school is in its first year of operation or its 150th, complete the dissolution section with great care. Like every other section, review this one regularly for its continued legal and institutional accuracy and appropriateness.

A sample of a sound dissolution section follows.

Article XII: Dissolution

In the event of the dissolution or final liquidation of the corporation, none of the property of the corporation nor any of the proceeds shall be distributed to or divided among any of the Trustees or inure to the benefit of any individual. After all liabilities and obligations of the corporation have been paid, satisfied, and discharged, or adequate provision has been made therefor, all remaining property and assets of the corporation shall be distributed to one or more nonprofit organizations that meet the following criteria.

- *Such organizations shall be organized and operated exclusively for charitable, scientific, research, or educational purposes.*
- *Transfers of property to such organizations shall, to the extent then permitted under the statutes of the United States, be exempt from federal gift, succession, inheritance, estate, or death taxes (by whatever name called).*

> ▪ *Such organizations shall be exempt from federal income taxes by reason of section 501(c)(3) of the Internal Revenue Code of 1954 (or the corresponding provision of any subsequent federal tax law).*

Your Board's version of this simple, straightforward statement must be included in your bylaws for them to become a complete and organizationally responsible document. The intent of the section is obvious: to ensure that no individuals profit from the closure of a school and to guarantee, as possible, that charitable organizations receive the school's assets without inappropriate taxation.

When reviewing your bylaws' dissolution section, take the opportunity similarly to ensure that a section exists specifying the necessary steps for bylaw alteration. Frequently included as the penultimate section, ISM suggests the following or similar language.

> **Article XI: Amendment and Review of the Bylaws**
>
> *New bylaws may be adopted or these bylaws amended or repealed by an affirmative vote of two-thirds of the full Board, provided the proposed changes are distributed to the full Board 30 days before any meeting at which changes are to be considered.*

Altering bylaws or adopting new ones should not, as an organizational process, be made impossibly cumbersome. Yet the seriousness of any such change does imply the inclusion of a bylaw statement that alterations must be accomplished in a manner that assures a chance for thoughtful deliberation involving all Trustees. Furthermore, more than a simple majority should be required to effect the changes.

Board Policies

The Board of Trustees must always be mindful of the need to perpetuate Board memory—historical information about the Board's operations and activities. Even with effective Board new-member orientation and annual professional development, turnover will mean that, in a few years, most of the Board will rely on secondhand information about "how the Board does things." Trustees may not have experienced the passage of some pivotal Board policies or discussion about the Board's strategic operation. When they join the Board, the new Trustees often rely on what they "heard" from the more experienced Board members.

It is better to rely on a stored record of the Board's operational policies and practices than it is to count on individual memory. Every Board should have a Board Policy Manual—a loose-leaf binder that is given to each Trustee, an electronic document, or both. Whatever the form, this manual provides each

Trustee a ready reference for the important documents concerning the Board and its operations and strategic practices.

The Board Policy Manual

The manual should contain the following sections.

- **Mission and Purpose and Outcome Statements** (see Chapter Six): Place the school's mission and Board's mission at or near the front. These documents provide the Board with guidance on why the Trustees meet and make decisions (school mission) and about the long-term, strategic frame of reference (Board mission). With the mission statements, include two other definitive documents—a Portrait of the Graduate (a list of desired student outcomes) and Characteristics of Professional Excellence (a list of characteristics serving as an operational definition of your faculty "ideal").

- **Strategic Plan and Strategic Financial Plan** (see Chapter Four): Include the current strategic plan—with the time-lined goals, costs and revenue sources, and responsible entity noted. To detail the goals, provide the Board's annual agenda, noting the committee responsible for each item on the agenda and the date the committee will report to the Board. Clearly delineate charges for each committee. The annual administration agenda follows, highlighting any administrative goals that will involve Board participation.

Each year, update the manual. Include a record of accomplished goals, as well as any documents that show goals considered for inclusion in the plan but omitted. Often, as resources become available, schools find they can attend to some of these second-level goals.

- **Operations Budget:** The first page of this section should be the strategic financial plan, the document that guides operations budget preparation and implementation. Behind that, include a one-page summary of the current annual budget, noting major revenue and expense accounts.

- **Calendar:** The calendar includes a list of the meeting dates and the topic(s) to be brought forward by a committee for each meeting. Directly tie the calendar to the Board's annual agenda and committee charges.

- **Lists:** Include the names of all Trustees in this section—their spouses or partners, if applicable, and contact information. Just behind this, include a list of all Board committees for that year, with the members (including contact information for any non-Board members of each committee).

- **Board Policies:** Include all Board policies still in effect in this section.

- **Meeting Minutes:** First, include the Board meeting minutes, with all passed resolutions signified in bold print so they will be easy to identify. Transfer the minutes to the section on Board policies during the annual updating. Follow this with minutes from all committee meetings.
- **Head's Reports:** Copies of the Head's reports provide a historical record of the important events in school life—ones the Head felt the Board should know about. As the year progresses, it may be helpful to have these reports to refer to during meetings.
- **Board Evaluation:** Board evaluation demonstrates where to strengthen the Board's strategic operations. Copies of past Board evaluations will be helpful to the Committee on Trustees as it measures progress on Board professional development goals and evaluates future goals based on the strategic plan.
- **Bylaws and Amendments:** The bylaws (with the date of passage) and subsequent amendments (with their dates of passage) are documents that need to be at hand during all official Board and committee meetings.
- **Marketing Message:** The Advancement Team develops this one-page summary. This summary ensures that, as individual Trustees fulfill their ambassadorial role, they are all giving consistent and accurate messages and, thus, effectively supporting the internal and external marketing efforts.
- **Statistics:** Often, statistical data like enrollment, recruitment and re-recruitment, and development information are more appropriately the province of the administration and require no Board action. Include all such information in the manual for reference.

A Board Policy Manual will help address many concerns about Board operations and the policies and practices that undergird those operations. The written record accurately carries forward the information and documents needed to ensure consistent year-to-year Board activity.

Conflict-of-Interest Policies

Over the years, ISM Consultants have worked with many private schools that have faced conflict-of-interest issues. Such problems usually occur because a school has not (or has not properly) written a policy.

As a 501(c)(3) institution, your school should abide by the format developed by the Internal Revenue Service for creating such a policy. As part of your fiscal stewardship, make sure your school has a comprehensive policy. Use the following headings and components to organize your document, customize the content to fit the needs of your school, and then have your school's legal counsel review it.

Purpose

A clearly articulated purpose statement is the foundation of an excellent conflict-of-interest policy. Include language that protects the school's interests when entering a transaction or arrangement that might benefit the private interest of a Trustee, school employee, or other interested party.

Definitions

Your policy statement requires definition of two basic terms.

- **Interested Person:** Any Trustee, principal officer, employee, or family member (defined as a spouse, child, or household member) who has a direct or indirect financial interest in a transaction or arrangement with the school has a potential conflict of interest. (For the rest of this chapter, we'll call this individual the "Interested Person.")

- **Financial Interest:** A financial interest occurs when ownership or investment interest is held by an Interested Person, when compensation occurs, or when potential ownership or investment interest is present by an Interested Person. Compensation means direct and indirect remuneration as well as gifts or favors. In plain words, if an Interested Person either directly or indirectly benefits from a transaction that occurs with an organization for which he or she volunteers or works, there may be a conflict of interest.

However, a financial interest is not necessarily a conflict of interest. The Board must develop guidelines to determine when a conflict exists; clarity is essential. Boards must have clear conflict-of-interest disclosure policies that outline potential conflicts, explain how conflicts of interest are determined, and dictate requirements for Interested Persons to disclose them. Failure to do so can cause serious issues, including the loss of 501(c)(3) status for nonprofit schools.

Procedures

This section of your conflict-of-interest policy explains the protocol of the policy.

Record of Proceedings

The minutes of the Board should reflect the name(s) of the person(s) who disclosed a potential conflict of interest, the nature of the interest, any action taken to determine whether a conflict was present, and the Board's final decision. Also, record the names of the Trustees present for discussions and votes.

Compensation

A voting member of the Board who is found to be in a conflict of interest, or a Trustee who receives compensation directly or indirectly from the school, is precluded from voting on matters pertaining to his or her compensation. A voting member of the Board or any committee whose jurisdiction includes compensation, directly or indirectly, from the organization is not prohibited from providing information to any committee regarding compensation.

Annual Statement

Each Trustee, committee member, and employee (especially personnel involved with the school budget) must annually sign a statement that affirms he or she:

- has received a copy of the conflict-of-interest policy;
- has read and understands the document;
- has agreed to comply with the policy; and
- understands the school is a 501(c)3 organization and, to maintain its federal tax exemption, must engage primarily in activities that accomplish its mission.

Periodic Reviews

To ensure that your school operates in a manner consistent with charitable purposes and does not engage in activities that could lead to jeopardizing its tax-exempt status, conduct periodic reviews of your policy.

Use of Outside Experts

The use of outside experts is allowed but does not absolve the Board from the responsibility of ensuring that periodic reviews are conducted.

Conclusion

While a conflict-of-interest policy may seem unnecessary, think through a policy position before a conflict occurs. This will protect the school from unnecessary stress and may ultimately preserve the school's tax-exempt status.

This chapter does not constitute legal advice. Have your legal counsel review your policy statement to ensure that you are compliant with all relevant federal and state tax laws.

Contents of a Board Handbook

With term limits for members, over a relatively short period of time (five to six years), the Board's composition can change, resulting in an almost completely new Board. In their earlier years on the Board, current members relied on what they "heard" from the more experienced members about the Board's operational practices. Over time, the rationale behind a practice can be forgotten. To address this gap in the institutional memory, charge an ad hoc committee with creating a Board Handbook. This ad hoc committee of former and current Trustees should include the Chair of the Committee on Trustees (as a member, but not Chair). A former Board President or committee Chair might be selected to lead this committee, which will have a lifespan of a couple of months.

Properly developed, a Board Handbook becomes a useful tool for many aspects of the Board's functions. It is a "textbook" for new-Trustee orientation, as well as a reference book for committee and Board meetings, and the definitive guide to "how we do things on the Board."

Give the Committee on Trustees Chair the following content list of what the handbook should contain. Encourage the Chair to include topics that are important in the Board's current duties. Put the book in a loose-leaf binder and have labeled dividers between each section. This manual should contain:

- both the school and the Board mission statements;
- the expectations of Trustees (e.g., preparation for meetings; on-time attendance at all meetings; full participation in meetings; personal financial contributions promptly made in support of all fundraising goals; serious commitment to the confidentiality of Board matters; enthusiastic support publicly for the school, its faculty, its Head, and each Trustee's own Board colleagues);
- a member list, noting each Trustee's profession, family members, affiliation with the school (past parent, alumnus, previous Board member), and contact information;
- the Board bylaws;
- the current strategic plan and strategic financial plan;
- the long-range plan (and any other current plan: development, marketing, technology);
- the annual operating budget;
- the most recent audit;

- minutes from Board and committee meetings, with attachments (to facilitate finding policies, ask the Secretary to put all passed motions in bold);
- policies, arranged by topic (financial, development, Board evaluation);
- the annual agenda;
- the Board's annual calendar;
- the school calendar;
- a list of those responsible for each administrative task at the school;
- the school profile—a "just-the-facts" listing of key programs, statistics, and data that is a versatile, economical marketing tool;
- the recruitment brochure and annual report; and
- copies of the current year's newsletters. (These last three items help the Board members fulfill their ambassador function for the school, giving them ready information to share with others.)

Distribute the handbook during orientation of new Trustees and review each section. Ask all members to bring their handbooks to Board meetings. Then, if there is a question about how the Board operates, that section of the handbook can be consulted. In addition, when the agenda packet is sent out before the Board meeting, important documents (e.g., a budget update, minutes from the previous meeting, or a committee's proposal to be acted on) can be put in the handbook. This makes it easier for Trustees to have everything they need during the meeting.

A Board handbook provides a ready reference for past actions, supplies a guide to how the Board operates, becomes a dependable institutional memory, and can help streamline meetings.

CHAPTER THREE

Understanding Private School Finances

Financial Equilibrium: The Three 'Levers'

Private school finances are simple. That's not to say the Finance Committee doesn't have complex matters to deal with, from budgeting to gift management to investing strategies. But the basis of it all is straightforward, and every Trustee must understand it at least at this level. Any strategic plan not grounded in realistic financial specifics is not a plan at all. It's a "wish list," and its chances of coming to pass are poor.

When the school's Trustees, School Head, and senior administrators get together for the once-every-four-years strategic planning process, you must ensure that your school maintains its financial equilibrium. That's determined by three financial components. Visualize them as "levers," each of which interacts with the others.

Lever No. 1: Your Employee Compensation Package
Salaries and benefits comprise the major portion of your operating expenses, probably between 65% and 75%. (Your next biggest line is probably financial aid, and everything else is pretty much a fixed cost—utilities, maintenance, and so on.)

 Lever No. 2: Hard Income
Hard income is your net tuition and fees, coupled with any earned interest (e.g., from cash reserves) and any "profit" from auxiliary programs (such as a summer camp and extended care).

 Lever No. 3: Your Student-Staff Ratio
The number of people who are paying you, compared with the number of people you are paying, equals the student-staff ratio.

That's it. Three levers. Deciding where to set each one may turn out to be a tough task, but it's not complex. You set those three levers when, during the strategic planning process, you and your colleagues:

– brainstorm your "ideal school" four to six years into the future,

– place expense estimates on all your new items (such as an additional secretarial position or employee benefit), and

– take a look at what this version of your school will cost to operate.

That's strategic planning and strategic financial planning, both done, of necessity, at the same time. If you are tempted to name a fourth lever, let go of the idea.

That fourth one can only be "soft money"—that is, dollars that you solicit. It's risky business to construct your strategic financial future around asking for money, as distinct from charging for your services.

Fundraising (as an outcome of good development) is in itself a great thing—as long as you're not asking for money to run the school for salaries, benefits, and utilities. Ask for money, instead, for enhancements and capital improvements and projects. People stretch their checkbooks to support specific enhancements that increase the school's value to them—playground equipment, a software package for a science program, or uniforms for the softball team. Helping you balance the budget is simply not an exciting prospect for most people.

When the Levers Move

Here's the thing: Those levers you set on your planning day are connected. When you move one lever, the gears (which are out of your sight) start grinding against one another, attempting to move the other levers without your touching them. If your finances are in equilibrium (if your budget balances without Development Office assistance), moving Lever No. 1 forward (to pay for salary and benefit increases) means that Levers No. 2 and No. 3 will strain to compensate. Otherwise, your budget will immediately move out of equilibrium.

Your school four to six years from now will cost more to operate than it does now (a virtual certainty). Just know there are two ways to pay for that. You can increase tuition, fees, interest income, or auxiliary profit. Or you can increase the number of students in each classroom, which shifts the student-staff ratio. (There is a third way—make your teachers teach more classes, but that seems an obvious nonstarter.)

Everyone would like to set the levers to have the highest possible salaries and employee benefits (Lever No. 1), the lowest possible tuition (Lever No. 2), and the lowest possible student-staff ratio (Lever No. 3).

Here's how that equation works out:

> High Compensation + Low Tuition + Low Ratio = Bankruptcy

Like all such algebraic phenomena, the equation is unforgiving. If you force one lever to move substantially in a particular direction and then do not allow the others to move in compensating directions, expect to glide down one of the slipperiest slopes in all of private school operations. Insolvency awaits your school, and it may not take long to get there.

Strategic planning is hard work, not because it is complicated, but because it demands courage from the planners. You must coordinate your vision of the "ideal school" with the fiscal realities, and then make the tough decisions that keep the levers working in sync. That way, you ensure the financial equilibrium that allows your school to deliver its mission, maintain viability, and sustain educational excellence.

The Concept of Price, Product, and Process

ISM has long urged private school leaders to agree among themselves that their school operates—or intends to operate—with one of three marketplace focuses: price-value, best-product, or best-process. In its simplest terms:

- price-value focus means that your primary (not your only) case for enrollment is your affordability;

- best-product focus means that your primary (not your only) case for enrollment is your academic superiority; and
- best-process focus means that your primary (not your only) case for enrollment is that you offer more programs at more levels (i.e., more individualization) than do your competitors.

More can be said about each of these, but those definitions will serve as an adequate starting point for this discussion. To understand the finances of your school, the Board must first come to terms with this concept and where your school stands in the marketplace.

Your regularly scheduled strategic planning and strategic financial planning event calls for clarity, as you move into the planning sessions, regarding your intended marketplace focus. Consider, for example, if your core marketplace focus is your affordability. You will make a costly mistake—"costly" in more ways than one—if you add substantially to the number of your student programs or to the levels within those programs. If you do either or both of those, your expenses will rise sharply and tuition levels will follow. Your new strategic plan will move you away from your core affordability focus and toward the focal points adopted by schools in the other two marketplace categories.

Adding to your programs or to the levels within those programs, aside from increased expense and tuition levels, places your school conceptually on the same playing field with the "best-process" schools (with which you do not primarily compete). You will be moving toward using their rules, their systems, their goals, their salaries, their faculty characteristics, their expenses, and their tuition.

From this one example, you can see the question of which marketplace focus is "best" has no meaning. The point of the tripartite distinction is that, by knowing, understanding, and formulating your strategic plan and strategic financial plan with an appropriate marketplace focus, you can remain consistent in your approaches to staffing, expenditures, tuition levels, tuition assistance, and all else that goes with those elements. The resulting plan will be a coherent expression of the marketplace focus that best fits your school's intended purposes and outcomes.

Examine the following table and consider its implications for your school, especially with regard to your next strategic planning and strategic financial planning event—whether scheduled soon or several years from now.

Marketplace Focus	Accessibility	Academic Product	Individualization
Admission Selectivity	Values-based	Ability-based	Broad-based
Costs to Market	Low	High	High
Student-Staff Ratio	High	Midrange	Low
Programmatic Focus	Targeted outcomes	Targeted outcomes	Breadth of outcomes
Outcome Characteristics	Best prepared for values-driven life	Best prepared for next academic level	Best prepared for creating one's own path

Private schools can, in some marketplaces, compete simultaneously and successfully based on "academic product" and "individualization." Such schools may consequently become even more expensive than schools that compete based on one or the other. For example, such a PK–12 school would likely need an extensive next-level-placement counseling staff in the upper school and an extensive personal counseling staff, rather than emphasizing one type of counseling staff over the other.

In contrast, few private schools can compete simultaneously and successfully with "accessibility" on the one hand, and "academic product" or "individualization" on the other. Accessibility-focused schools can compete simultaneously and successfully, however, with "academic product" or "individualization" against other private schools within their own price range, i.e., within the "accessibility" category itself. Your accessibility-focused school can write its new strategic plan and strategic financial plan with the goal of achieving or maintaining a "best product" or "most thoroughly individualized" stance when compared specifically with other accessibility-focused schools.

It follows that, whatever your marketplace focus, your marketing materials—Purpose and Outcome Statements (see Chapter Six), distinguishing descriptors, website claims—must carefully circumscribe the claims you choose to make. For an accessibility-focused school to make the unqualified claim to have the "best academic product" (graduates best prepared for next academic level) or "most thoroughly individualized programs" (students best prepared to create their own path now and in the future) risks exposure by comparison with true best-product and most-individualized schools' standardized test scores and student-staff ratios.

Study your true competitors in the marketplace. Analyze their characteristics, using the ingredients in the table on the previous page. Come to a decision about your most advantageous competitive focus. Then launch your strategic planning and strategic financial planning event with confidence that your planning decisions will systematically strengthen your position in your marketplace.

Governance and Fiscal Vigilance

Trustees must set policies to ensure the financial soundness of the school's assets—and monitor the application of these procedures. Each should be on a rotation for review, examining and reaffirming all policies within a five-year cycle.

Don't limit new-Trustee orientation to focusing on the Board's primary role of strategic thinking and planning. Expand it to include a thorough discussion of all policies set by the Board. All Trustees must be conversant with the policies, how they are applied, and how the Board oversees their application and effectiveness.

Well-managed schools will have policies that address the requirement to have a financial audit annually and a risk management audit every five years. Other key management guidance tools that must be in place and reviewed regularly by appropriate Board committees include:

- the delineation and application of key accounting precepts;
- banking policies and practices—especially concerning receipt of funds (tuition and all other income) and cash management;
- tuition assistance policies;
- employment policies and practices;
- gift acceptance and management policies;
- endowment investment management and spending policies; and
- facilities management policies and practices.

Trustees with certain expertise can guide the process of setting policies and evaluating the effectiveness of their implementation. While audit and banking policies are specific, other school policies and practices are harder to oversee. However, they are no less important in protecting the school.

Let us look at each key policy to determine the proper methods Trustees may use to ensure that each is implemented as intended.

Annual Audit Policy
- Actively involve the Board in selecting or re-engaging the school's audit firm.
- Review the test parameters with the audit firm. What is the dollar threshold for testing receivables, purchasing authorization, payables, capitalization, etc.?
- Share your financial policies with the audit firm; ask auditors to affirm that your policies are being practiced.
- Question changes in assets and liabilities when the draft of the audit report is received. Determine whether significant changes were reported to the Board as they occurred throughout the year.
- Question the variances if the Statement of Financial Activities varies significantly from the regular reports received by the Board. Be sure the explanations fit with your understanding of the events that took place during the year.
- Have the Board committee charged with receiving the audit report go into executive session (Head and Chief Financial Officer will not be present) with the audit firm representatives. Ask these representatives if they observed any questionable practices or indications of malfeasance. (While an audit management letter usually contains such observations, Boards often stop with the audit report and do not take the time to study this important document.)
- Ask the Head and Business Manager to draft a response to the audit management letter and review the draft response to be sure the concerns raised have been addressed to the satisfaction of the Trustees.

Banking and Cash Management Policies

Update the bank resolutions on file with each financial institution. Bank resolutions define who can sign checks or sell stocks for the school. With any change in Board officers or management personnel who have such authority, file new banking resolutions within two weeks.

Other steps the Board can take include:
- reviewing the school's funds deposit and withdrawal policy. How often are funds to be deposited—daily, two, or three times weekly? Will you require more than one signature on checks? Will you require the signature of a Trustee on checks over a certain amount?

– examining the process for completing bank statement reconciliations: Who reviews these? Are the statements reconciled in the specified time?

– reviewing of your cash management policies and practices at least every two years. This assessment should confirm the types of financial instruments in which the Chief Financial Officer may invest the school's short-term funds. The policy should also specify whether the Chief Financial Officer has full authority to transfer funds between the school's checking and investment account(s), or whether such action would require the approval of the Treasurer.

In dealing with nonfinancial school policies and practices, there is no one-size-fits-all answer. Each school should consider the best way to monitor its accountability to its stakeholders. We offer the following suggestions, which can form the basis of developing an accountability protocol.

Tuition Assistance Policy

For many schools, tuition assistance (financial aid) represents a significant cost of doing business. Trustees should familiarize themselves with the policies the school has in place and determine whether those policies support both the school's mission and its strategic objectives. Because tuition assistance is confidential, Trustees cannot directly monitor whether the policy is being implemented in the manner intended.

One solution is to ask the school's auditor to review several tuition assistance applications. Is the policy being applied fairly and cost-effectively?

Employment Policies and Practices

The employment area is complicated, and problems in this area have the greatest potential to damage the school's reputation. Trustees typically can provide expertise and guidance in this important area of school management.

Oversee a review of the school's employment policies and practices in any year in which those policies and practices have changed. Entrust the task to an ad hoc committee (Personnel Committee or Policy Review Committee) charged with their review.

Gift Acceptance and Management Policies

Every school should have a gift acceptance policy. The Development Committee should review this policy within the five-year policy rotation and reconfirm or amend the procedure. A few schools have even codified their gift management policy and procedure; this policy would specify such elements as the proper disposition of stock gifts to the school. Who has the authority to receive them? Should they be sold or held in the school's investment account? How will these gifts be recorded in the school's financial records?

Endowment Investment Management and Spending Policies

One of the Board's primary responsibilities is to nurture and manage the school's endowment fund so it will be available to support the school's mission across generations of students.

The Board has the duty to determine and complete a fiscally prudent investment policy, and hire investment managers who can implement the policy to produce the desired results. Scrutiny of the investment policy and practice by Trustees who are not members of the Investment Committee can provide a useful check and balance in monitoring the investment process. Encourage Trustees to question results that appear out of line with their general perceptions of the expected outcomes.

Facilities Management Policies and Practices

Your facilities exist to fulfill mission by supporting programs and services. Developing policies and practices designed to preserve these facilities is another important role for Trustees. A typical policy provides a source of ongoing funding to maintain and upgrade existing facilities. The policy should establish a benchmark for funding repairs and replacement. This fund is generally called Provision for Plant Renewal, Replacement, and Special Maintenance (PPRRSM). Many schools determine their funding model based on a percentage of the replacement value of the facilities, usually 2.0% to 2.5%.

Schools are encouraged to maintain an updated long-range property plan and Campus Master Development Plan.

Due diligence is an ongoing process for Trustees. Asking tough questions, examining and thoughtfully considering the answers provided, and adjusting policies and practices when and where necessary, are all part of holding the mission of the school in trust. When the Board focuses on its due diligence responsibility, the school's stakeholders will have no or little need to question the Board about the appropriateness of its actions.

Financial Aid: The Board's Responsibility

Let's zero in on financial aid policy, based on your school's particular mission and budget guidelines—careful calculations of per-pupil cost, retained earnings, and incremental costs.

To develop an effective financial aid policy, your Board must:

1. **Decide on the specific, mission-based purposes of aid at your school.** Although basic policy can be temporarily amended to reflect new situations, your financial aid policy should remain intact—something that a Trustee "buys" on accepting Board membership.

2. **Evaluate the different types of aid: need-based and non-need-based aid, loans, merit scholarships, and tuition reimbursement or reduction.** Your Board must decide what the proper "blend" of financial aid should be at your school and have a policy statement that reflects that decision.

3. **Specify the amount allocated in total and to each type of aid.** Some schools determine the total amount of aid available by basing it on a specific number of tuitions. Other schools allocate a fixed percentage of budgeted tuition revenue or a percentage of total operating expenses. Most schools devote at least 8% of tuition revenue or about 10% of operating expense to financial aid.

4. **Determine which application process your school will use.** Require families to apply for aid every year. Some schools design their own application forms, and others prefer to use of Financial Aid for Student Tuition (FAST), an ISM service.

5. **Stipulate guidelines for awards.** They may be revised year-to-year, depending on your particular school's situation. For example, you may provide aid by grade, or you may decide to award aid by a percentage of need. Or you may even require all families to pay some tuition, perhaps a minimum of $500.

6. **Develop guidelines concerning the acceptance of late-summer applicants for aid.** If seats still need to be filled, marginal income is better than no income at all. Accepting late applicants can benefit all parties, as long as guidelines provided by the Board are observed.

Appropriate guidelines will streamline the financial aid process, make the best use of available funds, and ensure your classes are filled with mission-appropriate students.

CHAPTER FOUR

Strategic Planning and Strategic Financial Planning

The Difference Between 'Strategic' and 'Operational'

The business of a school is in its classrooms.

Many intelligent, well-intentioned Trustees infer the Board's business, too, should focus on day-to-day school operations. Consider the consequences of this notion, whether you currently observe it on your Board or fear it may develop. Typical ramifications include the following.

- Board meetings are dominated by:
    - a School Head report on current school events and issues, with particular attention to any developing classroom and curricular matters;

- reports from Board committees dealing with the oversight, evaluation, monitoring, and enhancement of curriculum and of teaching and coaching personnel; and

- reports from other Board committees dealing with student programs and personnel that are not classroom-specific (such as athletics and coaches).

- The Board becomes dominated by educators. The Board then places the greatest emphasis on those committees dealing with academic programs and curriculum; on character-development programs; and on the evaluation, oversight, and development the faculty, the teacher support staff, and the coaching staff.

- Institutional support functions, e.g., grounds and facilities, operations finance, and advancement (fundraising, communications, marketing, and student recruitment) are left to the administration, since they are secondary in importance. The Board can then focus on delivering services to students.

ISM observes that a significant minority of Trustees gravitate toward this education-focused version of trusteeship rather than toward the strategic approach. The rationale is that this curriculum and instruction focus should constitute "the Board's business." As parents of current students, Trustees find themselves drawn emotionally and intuitively toward the curriculum and the classrooms. Even within the best, most disciplined Boards, organizational schizophrenia can develop a psychological tug-of-war within, between, and among Trustees regarding where to focus the Board's efforts.

Strategic Versus Operations: What's the Difference?

Let's revisit this topic. When Boards stray into the operational realm, the result is almost always bad for the school. If they stay in the strategic realm and act in a mission-appropriate way, it's almost always good for the school.

What's the bridge between "strategicness" and operations? The School Head! That's the top reason the relationship between the Board of Trustees and the School Head is critical. Oversee the separation of strategic responsibilities and operations responsibilities to ensure that it stays healthy. The following table gives a sample of what this can look like.

Are there gray areas? Yes, nothing is ever quite as clear as we might like it. Don't sweat the perfect answer. Ensure that whatever the Board is looking after has a strategic importance, while giving the School Head autonomy and authority to run the school.

Strategic Responsibilities (Board)	Operations Responsibilities (School Head)
School mission (approval of any mission and philosophy statements)	School mission (delivered to the students) *This and the following two items are called Purpose and Outcomes Statements. (See Chapter Six for more information.)*
Strategic plan	Characteristics of Professional Excellence
Strategic financial plan	Portrait of the Graduate
Annual Board agenda	Annual administration agenda
School Head evaluation, hiring, and firing	Faculty and staff evaluation, hiring, and firing
Budget (broad categories) and tuition-setting	Budget—how the money is allocated and disbursed line by line
Facilities planning, construction, renovation	Facilities maintenance
Master Campus Development Plan	Facilities audit
Marketing plan and parent retention and education plan	Marketing plan and parent retention and education plan implementation
None in curriculum	Curriculum—content, how it's taught, and materials used
Leadership in development	Development Office management
Major gifts	Annual fund
Appropriate funding of professional development	Establishing a growth-focused faculty culture

Note: This should not be construed to mean the Head has no business in the strategic realm. On the contrary, the Head's vision informs strategic planning. The Head and the Leadership Team, by the Head's invitation, are integral to successful strategic planning and strategic financial planning.

Which Perspective is 'True'?

One set of competing inferences suggests the Board must organize itself to focus mainly on student programs. ISM's set of inferences comprises the near-opposite of this. Since "the business of a school is in its classrooms," the Board must focus everywhere except there. Emphasize:

- strategic planning;
- strategic finance:
- strategic profiling of the Board itself;
- strategic analyses of property and facilities;
- the Board-level major gifts program; and
- other noncurrent events, noncurriculum, nonclassroom, nonteaching, and coaching personnel issues. Operations-level emergencies may drive the Board onto the operating plane, but not often. The stronger and better established the strategic framework, the less often such emergencies occur.

The strategically focused Board can determine conditions of institutional and financial stability. Those conditions allow administrators and teachers to provide and sustain mission-specific excellence in classrooms, in curricula, and in the teaching and coaching ranks. *Boards that concentrate on current events, curriculum, and classrooms inevitably become embroiled in tense, divisive, and counterproductive efforts. They must avoid doing what academic administrations and faculties devote their lives and their careers to—establishing and maintaining outstanding, mission-specific, mission-appropriate teaching and learning conditions within stable, financially strong strategic frameworks.*

Your Board can manage any change in an organizationally productive way via strategic planning, supporting the School Head (who was hired to handle school operations), and developing policies that make clear the distinctions.

If there is no Board-level policy regarding Trustee discussion outside the boardroom of school-related topics, a written policy can reduce whatever disparity prevails on your Board. Even disciplined Trustees struggle to "stay out of it" (i.e., out of classroom- and faculty-targeted complaining and gossiping, and pervasive complaints from parents of current students), whether on the phone or in the parking lot. The policy need only state that the Board is not a grievance body—address classroom issues through the protocol of teacher first, academic administration next, School Head last. Publish the policy in your newsletter and on your website. Include the policy statement in your parent and student handbook. Encourage Trustees to cite the policy in their discussions, and to use it to maintain a non-classroom, strategic focus. Words are "heard differently" when spoken by a Trustee to a non-Trustee. The policy underscores that truth.

The Board's Two Primary Responsibilities

No matter how conscientious and well-intentioned, Trustees (and the Board as a whole) must continuously guard against involvement in day-to-day school management. When the Board allows its responsibilities to cross over into the school's operating plane, it creates a major obstacle to building and maintaining a healthy, harmonious Board-Head relationship.

Regardless of how well a school defines the various roles of the Board, the members must understand to whom and to what the Board is truly responsible. The Board's constituency does not comprise current students, parents, faculty, or administrators. Trustees must keep in mind that their charge is to maintain the essential character and integrity of the institution and ensure that it remains viable to serve the children of today's students.

Within this clear mindset, what then are the Board's two primary responsibilities?

The Board is responsible for preserving the trust.
As delineated in the original charter, this responsibility is both private and public. It is private insofar as the Board's obligations are to those who choose to take part in the school's program. However, it is also public in that the school has been licensed by the state to provide services under the charter's stipulated conditions. In preserving the trust, the Board must always operate within the defined parameters of what fulfills "prudent man" guidelines. Fiscal integrity—present and future—is integral to this responsibility.

The Board's second responsibility is to itself.
While operational authority is properly delegated to the school's administration, under the School Head's direction, Trustees are legally responsible for the school, and all legal liabilities rest with the Board. As a result, to protect the school, the Board must protect itself collectively and its members individually. Above and beyond the protections granted by federal and state government, the Board must obtain sufficient Directors and Officers (D&O) insurance coverage and include appropriate indemnification language in the Board bylaws. Some

states have passed laws limiting the liability of volunteers, including Trustees, as has the federal government in the Volunteer Protection Act of 1997. Talk with your insurance broker about what risks your Board may be subject to in your particular state.

The Foundations of Strategic Planning

> *"Strategic planning? That's so old fashioned. We should do strategic thinking a year at a time and not tie ourselves down so tightly. We are in a change environment and have to be able to take advantage of opportunities as they arise. A strategic plan is just too rigid!"*

You may have heard comments like these from your fellow Trustees and other school leaders. The view of planning as a difficult, counterproductive, and even dangerous course of action is not uncommon … and partially true.

Planning can be problematic, particularly when a school tackles the process for the first time or is facing necessary far-reaching changes. The plan the school chooses, strategic or long-range, also has an effect. However, the concept that planning sets a school's course in stone is erroneous. An effective plan is a road map. At first, you set a course to follow, but along the way you may change your route or, rarely, rethink your destination. The plan provides a reference point, one that helps you make good decisions about your journey, and helps you avoid traveling in circles or getting thoroughly lost along the way.

The "take advantage of opportunities" portion of the above statement is a potential danger sign. A school can function based on day-to-day decisions and good fortune. However, to make progress, the school's leaders must have clear perspective on where the institution wants to be and how it's going to get there. Failure to plan leads to mediocrity, or worse. And while a school should of course be able to identify and take advantage of opportunity, to make that the typical process is to undermine the discipline and patience needed for our schools to flourish.

With a plan in place, you have guidelines for making the decisions that undergird your school's future. You can maximize available resources and use them most effectively. For example, if one of the goals is to increase the upper school enrollment by one section, that factor could impact your assessment of candidates for the Athletics Director or Dean of Students position. In hiring, you would focus on applicants with demonstrated experience in building programs rather than those who had primarily sustained them.

Your plan is an important tool that supports your parent and student communications efforts, effectively sells your school's goals and general direction to the school community, and provides the "case for support" to donors. Remember that parents want to know that when they place their child in your school, you will be around for that child's graduation—the plan provides them with significant assurance. So, planning is an obligation, one that your Board must accept bravely, whether the process is challenging or not.

Planning comes in two flavors: strategic and long-range. Note here that the following definitions are how ISM uses these terms. They are not definitive, but differentiate the two different ways to develop plans. We define them only to ensure understanding in the context of this book.

Similarities
- Both cover a time frame of four to six years.
- Both should be redone every four years.
- Both are designed to drive your Board and management activity, year by year.
- Both are focused on the planning benefits discussed above.

Differences
- **Process:** A strategic plan deals with viability-related issues—what the school needs to enhance its stability and solvency. Each school must determine its "ideal" for each item, adding to the list if necessary. The goal is to create a document of strategic plan items that will drive the school's efforts in the coming years. The resulting strategic plan provides your school's leaders at all levels with a framework for making all kinds of decisions, large and small. Within that framework, excellence in the classroom can be sustained because it can be paid for. This plan is carried out by the Board of Trustees and the School Head—usually with most or all members of the Leadership Team (those that report to the Head).

    A long-range plan, on the other hand, may be similar in its outcome to the strategic plan but is carried out in quite a different way. While the strategic plan can take as little as a month of preparation and five days of meetings, a long-range plan will take six months to a year. It involves most or all the school's constituencies in focus groups, planning meetings, and an attempt to gain the buy-in of the school community at large. This buy-in becomes necessary since the long-range constituency-based plan is going to be more ambitious and potentially cost a lot more money. Putting parents in a room (let alone students) and asking them what they want is an invitation to create a laundry list.

- **Length:** While a strategic plan is short (four to eight pages), a long-range plan may run 20 to 40 pages. Note that this difference has nothing to do with the time—both cover four to six years. Instead, the size of the written plans differs because of what each type attempts to accomplish. The long-range plan often deals with student programs and thus involves operations as well as strategic items. Dealing with student-program issues quickly makes for a very thick document.
- **Planning Group:** A strategic plan is a Board and School Head document. A long-range plan is a "constituency-based" document, leaning heavily on focus groups or retreat sessions.

Long-range planning, with its considerable logistical complexities, is reserved for times when the school is in an (enviably) strong financial position and thus can afford to be visionary in an expensive way. Most schools lack the budget, working hard to make compensation competitive, avoid deferred maintenance, and provide the richness of staff and faculty needed to support students. While ISM is not opposed to long-range planning, we believe that strategic planning is the core process.

Preparation for Strategic Planning

Good strategic plans always have the following characteristics.

- They are built on a prioritized list. Typical items might include establishing a cash reserve, initiating a facilities audit, or enhancing the faculty and staff employee benefits package.
- Each item is assigned to a responsible person or entity (e.g., Board of Trustees, School Head, Board committee).
- Item implementation is phased in over a multiyear time line (six years).
- Each item has a cost attached where necessary (the financial resources needed to implement the item).
- Each cost is provided with a revenue source, and there are only two for most schools in most situations: tuition and fundraising.
- Tuition-setting each year is based on a baseline tuition gradient—increase—of inflation plus 2% (the tuition increase needed to maintain the current level of excellence and richness of program).
- Actual tuition increase is the baseline tuition gradient plus strategic item costs.

- New items in the budget are always funded at 100% hard income (tuition and fees) unless they are one-time-only costs, which can be paid for via fundraising.
- The strategic plan is reviewed every year (to adjust as necessary) and rewritten every four years for another rolling six years.

Note: Hard income is composed almost entirely of tuition and fees. ISM accepts other hard income sources to be 50% of endowment draw. Individual schools may have their own unique sources of income such as rentals, summer program, and Federation grants (for Jewish schools). Soft income is fundraising donations.

Questions to Ask in Preparation for Strategic Planning

As you prepare for your Board's strategic planning session, answering the following questions can help you anticipate critical elements for consideration.

- Do we have a cash reserve? Do we have a facilities audit so we know what we need in the Provision for Plant Replacement, Renewal, and Special Maintenance (PPRRSM) fund? Do we have a Board policy for ensuring the cash reserve is funded and spent appropriately?
- Do we have debt? What are our principal and interest payments, and are they recognized as an operations expense? Do we use surpluses (after building our cash reserves) to reduce debt? Do we have a culture of philanthropy?
- Do we have an endowment? Do we have endowment-building policies? Do we have an endowment-spending policy? Are operating surpluses (after building cash reserves and reducing debt) used to help build the endowment corpus?
- Do we have a strategic plan and a strategic financial plan? What are their characteristics? How do those characteristics compare with the ISM list?
- Are the School Head and the members of the Head Support and Evaluation Committee talking to one another about the health of the faculty culture? Are they collecting data points to substantiate their conversation?
- How much is our operations expense? How much tuition (including fees, e.g., such as book, extended care, summer program, and so on) do we get? What is the Board policy about hard income?
- Is Trustee recruitment reactive (we have three vacancies—let's put together a list of names) or proactive (we have a pipeline of potential Trustees groomed to serve as the Board profile suggests)? Is there a Committee on Trustees to take on this responsibility as a year-round activity?

- Are there two or three other Board members of the Board who could become the Board President, if necessary?
- What percent of the budget is given to professional growth and renewal (benchmark is 2%)? Where is the school in terms of its competition on compensation (benchmark is within 95%)? What is the management structure for the support of faculty?
- When was the last time we received excellent instruction and direction about our jobs as Trustees? Is it ongoing? Did everyone attend to the training? Do my colleagues and I have a strategic orientation?
- When was the last time the school's Development Office called without asking me for money? Do I feel motivated to give less, to give the same amount, or to give more, if possible?
- Do our facilities enable us to deliver our mission? Do we have a facilities audit in place? Do we have a Campus Master Development Plan?
- What is the school's retention rate? Does our school have more mission-appropriate students applying than we have room for? How are we marketing the school to our current parents and students (internal marketing)?

Data Collection Prior

For years, ISM has urged six-year strategic plans be constructed every four years (i.e., a six-year planning horizon, but a quadrennial construction of a new six-year plan). Strategic plans—plans that focus on money (pricing, tuition assistance, development), organizational structures (student-staff ratios, faculty-administration ratios), and facilities (current and future)—are designed to (1) provide periodic opportunities to gather pertinent data from numerous sources, in one place and at the same time; and (2) look afresh at that data in the context of the school's strategic assumptions and premises. The result is a strategic platform (financial, organizational, physical) that is designed to make it possible to deliver your mission (purposes and outcomes) at the highest possible levels over time—that is, to continue to prosper in your competitive market.

A thorough data-collection and data-organization list would include consideration of the following items:

- audit report;
- current and proposed budgets;
- enrollment history (six years, by gender and grade level);

- attrition history (six years, by gender and grade level);
- tuition history (six years, adjusted for inflation);
- tuition-assistance history (six years, adjusted for inflation);
- survey of "referent" salaries ("referent": competing schools, association data, etc.);
- survey of "referent" benefits ("referent": competing schools, association data, etc.);
- survey of comparative tuitions (competing schools-association data);
- debt service and total debt data: six-year history;
- endowment levels: three-year history;
- property and facilities plan;
- property and facilities analysis;
- capital projects: proposals;
- capital-project history;
- fundraising levels (annual, not capital): six-year history (broken down into categories of givers);
- faculty professional development budget and history;
- survey of current parents (including demographic and income information);
- survey of past parents;
- attrition survey of past parents who left the school early;
- survey of young alumni;
- survey of adult alumni;
- survey of faculty;
- survey of nonteaching staff;
- survey of past Trustees;
- consumer Price Index assumptions and floor-gradient recommendation (CFO and Finance Committee);
- risk management assessment;
- accreditation document (executive summary and list of recommendations);
- self-scoring (within previous three months), using the ISM Stability Markers™ (see Chapter Five) Management proposal(s): e.g., (a)

recommendations on changes and additions in administrative structure; (b) student-staff ratio recommendations (e.g., class size changes, changes in number of sections for divisions, new programs); (c) faculty and staff salary gradient and approach; (d) benefits package; (e) advancement plan; and

- Strategic Board Assessment results and history (see Chapter Thirteen).

Strategic Continuity and Board Memory

Whether you're about to embark on your first strategic planning session or you've been doing strategic planning for decades, it is important to track your progress to ensure continuity. Over the years, ISM's onsite visits have uncovered a disconcertingly broad range of completeness in the organizational histories provided by school documents and by individuals' memories. Your school's "strategic history" provides both constraints and opportunities for its strategic future. Consider a formal review of the quality of your existing historical portrait, to reorganize that portrait, if needed, and elevate the quality of your school's organizational "Board memory."

As you develop a review approach, take the following steps to streamline the process.

- With your Committee on Trustees, add to your annual Board agenda an item such as: "Review Board and other documents and reorganize them, if needed, to establish strategic continuity in the organization's history."

- Convert this Board agenda item into a committee charge, with language such as: "By March 15 of next year, review pertinent strategic documents (e.g., Board minutes, planning documents, accreditation documents, incorporation documents, bylaws, policy manuals, audit statements, annual budgets, and strategic financial plans). Construct a strategic history in bullet-point format. Limit the document length to four pages with no more than 40 bullet points to maintain a 'big-picture' focus for its readers." (The Board President may give this charge to a pre-existing Board committee, but may decide that this task is sufficiently large and important to justify creating a new committee, one with a lifespan of about eight months.)

- Ensure the new committee Chair keeps the goal clearly in mind—a brief strategic history in bullet-point format, summarizing the past to highlight the (implied) constraints and opportunities affecting the organization's strategic future. Make sure the committee Chair is clear that, given that the Board of Trustees must operate fundamentally as a planning entity, a brief, accurate, user-friendly, strategic history is by definition a core Board document.

- As the March (in this example) task-completion deadline nears, write a single-page cover memo for the four-page document to the Trustees. This will accompany the strategic history document that will be sent to them 10 days before the Board meeting when the history will be discussed and presumably endorsed. In your memo, underscore the history's purpose: to provide a stronger foundation for the Board's regular strategic planning activities. Ensure the Trustees reading the history understand that it is short because it features only the major viability-related items in the school's past. It is not a complete history in any sense, but a Board tool to be used to strengthen planning activities.

Three Steps to Enhance Your Future Organizational Portrait

The Board may choose to institute measures now that will make future strategic history research efforts comparatively simple, enhancing future strategic planning efforts. The following are key steps to consider.

- Produce an annual set of "action minutes" from your Board meetings. A list of your Board's formal decisions, taken from the accumulated sets of full minutes, greatly simplifies creating any strategic history. If, appended to this (probably one-page) list, you also attach the single-page short-form operations budget and the six-year (also single-page) strategic financial plan, the strategic history compilation process will be streamlined still further.

- Every second year, write a single-page strategic history covering the tenure of the Board President. File this page in the same storage binder as the annual set of action minutes. Restrict your strategic history to a series of bullet points delineating only the most highly strategic events or outcomes (e.g., major gifts progress, cash-reserve levels, percent coverage of operations expense with hard income, size of applicant waiting pools at various levels).

- Have the Committee on Trustees, in its next Board profile, consider including one or even two slots for "recycled" Trustees. The committee may develop a profile slot specifically targeting a person who rotated off the Board one, several, or many years before, to boost the "institutional memory" physically present in your Board deliberations.

When the time comes to create your next strategic plan, use your updated strategic history in the same way that you use survey data, demographic data, and any other pertinent material assembled for review before the strategic planning retreat day. Arm your Board, School Head, and other leaders and planners with a concise list of the critical strategic events and benchmarks (positive and negative) from your school's past. Enter your planning cycle prepared to recreate the peak years of your institutional past—not by copying earlier decisions, but by studying them and shaping them to your school's present and future.

Strategic Financial Planning

A strategic financial plan projects operational income and expense figures over the time span of the strategic plan, allowing the Board to envision each planning item's financial implications within a realistic financial framework. Tuition is predicted forward.

In the summary, the strategic financial plan:

- covers the same length of time as the strategic plan,
- is a one-page document,
- assumes flat student numbers (i.e., no growth),
- assumes flat annual giving income (i.e., no growth), and
- measures the key components of strategic finances that all Trustees must understand, including cash reserves.

Without a Strategic Financial Plan ...

Without this document, your school invites some or all the following negative situations.

- The annual tuition-setting exercise may be nothing more than a painful, and often counterstrategic, debate concerning "How much are the parents willing to pay?" As a Trustee, you may well be one of those parents. The answer to the question is invariably, "Not much."

- The increase in faculty and staff compensation often becomes uncoupled from the tuition and hard-income package's upward gradient. Decisions on the compensation package are consequently shaped via another debate framed in language such as, "How much does the faculty need?" The answer, because most teachers are underpaid, is invariably, "A lot."

- The conservative nature of financial documents is overcome by the wishful thinking inherent in most optimistic student recruitment projections.

- Shortfalls are "covered" by the hope that another 20 or so students will show up.
- The strategically crucial issue of building and maintaining adequate levels of cash reserves, and of continuous attention to their full funding, is often seen as less important or even ignored.
- Trustees think in terms of the current year, not in terms of where the school needs to be in five or six years to fulfill its mission in changing circumstances and to remain competitive.
- Operations budgeting becomes reactive, not proactive, with the students typically at the losing end.
- Accreditation recommendations, almost always expensive and programmatic, are carried out enthusiastically, without any regard to their long-term impact on viability.
- The Development Director becomes the de facto source of all "needed" revenue by the increasing demand to "cover the gap" (a weak fundraising position), rather than the proactive source of funds to enhance the student's experience (which paradoxically enable the school to attract significantly more donations).

Strategic Financial Planning Rules

Why a strategic financial plan: A strategic plan is a brief, sequenced, Board-generated list of viability-related items to be undertaken in the coming four to six years. (A sample plan is shown on page 74.) Typical items might include establishing a cash reserve, initiating an endowment-building process, or enhancing the employee benefits package. Accompany the strategic plan with a single-page strategic financial plan that projects operational income and expense figures over an equivalent time span. This allows the Board to envision each planning item's financial implications within a realistic financial framework.

Enrollment: Enrollment projections should not exhibit growth unless rock-solid evidence exists to support such an increase. Your SFP should be a financially conservative document that does not "cheat"—i.e., allow avoidance of crucial financial decisions by simply projecting ever-higher enrollments as the route to solvency. Other forms of "cheating" include using line 3 or line 8 of your plan similarly, to show growth in nontuition revenues as a means of avoiding the core pricing and expense issues.

Financial Aid: Most private schools use unfunded tuition assistance to attain both full classrooms and socioeconomic diversity in the student body. "Unfunded" refers to tuition assistance that represents discounts from the listed tuition figure, as distinct from funded tuition assistance, which comes from interest generated by an endowment. Display your tuition revenue projections in your SFP as a net figure, after unfunded tuition assistance has been subtracted. In practice, this means that, to achieve the assumed net tuition revenue increase of inflation-plus-5.5%-per-year, actual annual tuition increases must exceed that figure. The tuition assistance allocation can then increase more than proportionally, allowing financially marginal families increased tuition assistance. (Note that financial aid includes discounts that may be provided to faculty children, multiparty discounts, and the like. ISM does not support this form of financial aid.

Operations Expense: Since the purpose of the plan is to provide a financial framework within which details are then set, a great deal of data must be collapsed into single lines. Accordingly, summarize operational expenses by a single line that captures every type of noncapital expenditure (including debt servicing—principal and interest).

Tuition and Expense Gradient Lines: The net tuition revenue gradient and the operations expense gradient form the key arithmetic relationship in your strategic financial plan. Because ISM data equate institutional stability with a high percentage of expenses covered by hard income, the income gradient should equal or exceed the expense gradient. Simply put, a school should never lose ground in this ratio. If the income gradient grows more rapidly than the expense gradient (by even 0.01% per year), this key relationship becomes "solvency-positive," and leads your school into a position of enhanced financial stability over time.

Tuition Setting: We find that many Boards and Leadership Teams construct the annual budget by asking questions such as, "How much more can the parent body stand?" or "How much more does the faculty need?" These are the wrong questions to ask. They ignore the purpose of operations finance: to fund the school that "we" (the Board, the Leadership Team, the faculty, the parent body, the students, the community) want eventually to sustain. The strategic question thereby becomes: "What will it cost to operate the school we want to have x years from now?" (Another way to put this is: "How much does it cost to deliver our mission to the students with excellence?")

Cash Reserves Line: Reserve funds incorporate unrestricted reserves, plant reserves, and other reserves (but not endowment) into a single figure, and compare that figure against one year's operations expenditures.

How Your Strategic Financial Plan Impacts Tuition Setting

Tuition setting is one of the Board's most difficult tasks. As an individual Trustee, particularly if you are a parent, talking about tuition (which you must do every year) can often be an exercise in frustration. Typical questions arise.

- How much did we raise tuition last year?
- How much does the competition charge?
- What can parents afford or are they willing to pay?
- What do you think our fundraising can produce?
- How do we keep our school affordable?

The simple answer is that none of these questions really matter, or at least they matter a lot less than this most strategic question: *Given our mission, what kind of education (and at what level of excellence) do we want to provide for our students?*

From a Trustee's perspective, you must approach tuition setting from a strategic and mission point of view. This means the following steps must be taken.

1. Develop a strategic plan. This will answer the question about how to sustain (and maybe improve) the excellence of the education being provided to the students.

2. Develop the accompanying strategic financial plan. This will tell you what the plan costs.

3. Market both to your "client." This respects the parent in the marketplace, creates transparency around the school's strategic direction and the financial situation, embraces the parent as a partner, and recognizes the Board's and school's responsibility to communicate.

What does all of this mean? The answer is that you can't win the dollars conversation. Ask parents what they want and the answer is, a lot. Ask them what they can afford to pay and the answer is, not much. That conversation goes nowhere.

However, when the conversation is around whether the school delivers value to the student—providing an exceptional academic education, or a truly transformative faith-based experience, or an incredible character-growth experience—that is a delightful conversation to be a part of. This is the value proposition conversation.

So tuition is about mission; parents' willingness to pay is based largely on their perception that they are receiving value. The marketing point is: Schools with value will always be attractive to parents. Money follows performance, when validated. Our research is clear that levels of tuition are idiosyncratic. It is also clear that parent satisfaction and student satisfaction is what creates great retention. So make your school the best it can be. That's your strategic task through your strategic plan. And that will enable your school to deliver excellence and thrive into the future.

Alternate Sources of Income

The Board wishes to develop alternate sources of income so the school becomes more "affordable." Is that realistic, and what might they be? Here are some ways to maximize the school's income.

- Ensure the Finance Committee really looks after the incoming monies well—interest on deposits can provide a nice supplement.
- Extended care programs (before and after school) provide both a valued service to the parent and an income stream.
- Courses that are offered after school (including adult education) by school personnel offer faculty an opportunity to derive additional income and also provide revenue for the school.
- Summer programs introduce potential students and faculty to the school, use the facilities efficiently, create additional income opportunities for faculty, and can bring in revenue for the school.
- Endowment funds can provide a steady revenue stream (except in market downturns!). Note, however, that endowment cannot and should not be used to depress tuition levels.

All of these are positive aspects of a school's overall programming, mission delivery, and income streams. None of them either individually or collectively will, for most private schools, ever be anything more than an adjunct to tuition. Tuition will remain the major source of income. So while these endeavors are unlikely to be bad, also understand the centrality of tuition and never waver from its strategic importance.

Product, Process, Price

As mentioned earlier in this book, your school competes in the marketplace (in a broad sense) based on one of three stances: product, process, or price.

You must take responsibility for assisting your colleagues in working from a marketplace stance that fits your school's actual competitive platform.

The Product School: To generate the best product (defined here as seeking to be academically the premier school in your market, producing the best academically prepared students—what might be termed college prep).

The Process School: To engage students in the best process (defined here as seeking to create a uniquely excellent physical and psychological learning environment). These schools might:

- engage in uniquely excellent pedagogical approaches;
- provide the greatest array of student curricular and cocurricular choice;
- achieve the lowest possible student-staff and student-faculty ratios; and
- demonstrate other process features that set the school apart based on the quality, quantity, and types of things it does every day.

The Price School: To be different from those schools that strive to be "the best" by product or process measures. Schools in this category can compete on the basis of their marketable differences and, because their marketplace stance is so "different," based on value and price. That is, they cost less than those schools in the first two categories because their priorities simply are not the same.

Which type school—product, process, or price—is the best? The question has no meaning when worded in that way. The distinction is this: If a difference-value-price school attempts to take on the characteristics of a product- or process-based school, its planning emphasis and outcome may become badly distorted. As a result, the plan would be expensive in ways it should not be, given the context.

Implications of Your Marketplace Stance

Identify your marketplace stance using this three-category taxonomy. You can then carry that stance into, and through, your quadrennial strategic planning and strategic financial planning process. The major ramifications are these.

If your marketplace stance is best product, you must accept that your school will be expensive. You will, for example, invest heavily in next-level placement programs. For example, in a PK–12 school, you will have a college counseling program that reaches well down into the middle school. In a PK–8 school, you will have a high school preparation program. And you will put time and effort into gathering product-specific data regarding your graduates: both quality of placement and quality of performance.

If your marketplace stance is best process, you must accept that your school will be even more expensive than best product schools. As implied in the earlier example, you will need the lowest possible student-staff and student-faculty ratios, an expensive arrangement in itself. You will need the widest possible array of curricular and cocurricular offerings, both technology-based and not (e.g., extensive differentiation among levels of sports teams, numerous foreign language offerings, state-of-the-art-plus instructional technology, and continual attention to this aspect of teaching and learning).

You will invest perhaps less than the product school in staffing your next-level-placement counseling program, but much more in staffing your personal counseling program. You will invest in diversity—an expensive proposition unless your approach excludes, for example, socioeconomic considerations. And you will offer diversity-related programs to accompany your emphasis on the make-up of your student body.

If your marketplace stance is your difference (translated here as best value or best price), then you will need, in your strategic planning and strategic financial planning events, to guard against your colleagues' understandable eagerness to plan as if you compete based on product or process. Said another way, this means that in planning, you focus on being "more yourself," with all the not necessarily costly differences that entails, and not "like" those schools in your area that compete based on product or process. If you do seek to emulate them, you will inadvertently weaken your school's basic marketplace stance by making it *considerably more expensive, and for the "wrong" kinds of reasons.*

The Marketplace Taxonomy: Overview

Schools can compete simultaneously based on product and process. Such schools become even more expensive than those schools that compete based on just product or just process. For example, such a PK–12 school would need an extensive next-level-placement counseling staff and an extensive personal counseling staff, rather than emphasizing one over the other.

In contrast, schools cannot compete simultaneously based on difference (defined here as including value or price) on the one hand, and based on product or process on the other. Difference-value-price-based schools can be relatively inexpensive and yet, at the same time, do a superb job of fulfilling their core reasons for existing. But they cannot effectively retain that marketplace stance and simultaneously seek to compete with product- or process-based marketplace competitors on their own turf.

Marketplace Stance and Tuition Implications

Take a look at the following table, which shows the kinds of dramatic differences in marketplace stance implied by the price, product, or process choice. The hypothetical school depicted is PK–12 with enrollment of roughly 700. The table illustrates a theoretical, ideal level of staffing, pricing, facilities, and, in general, performance against the ISM Stability Markers (see Chapter Five).

Characteristic	Price	Product	Process
Student-faculty ratio	16:1	10:1	8:1
Student-staff ratio	11.7:1	5.8:1	5.1:1
Tuition (2019 $)	$7K	$20K	$25K
Faculty	44	70	88
Administrators and staff	16	50	50

Major Dangers

Strategic planners (Board and senior administrators) in difference-value-price schools may seek to have product-process features without understanding the expense, and the probable loss of focus involved, as well, in shifting to a different marketplace stance. This creates a cost-value question in the marketplace.

Strategic planners (Board and senior administrators) in product schools may seek process features without understanding the expense involved in moving to that marketplace stance.

Strategic planners (Board and senior administrators) in process schools may continue to add such a plethora of programs and services that product (i.e., excellence of outcome) is compromised through sheer overload and faculty and staff exhaustion.

So look at your mission, determine what your marketplace stance is, decide what you want your school to continue to be or to become, and then set tuition based on those considerations. The result will be a school that delivers what it promises (its mission), validates the decision of parents and students to attend, and can sustain excellence over time because it charges the tuition needed.

Base Tuition Gradient

The tuition gradient is an important number for you to know. It is the amount that tuition must increase for the school to keep what it has now at the same level of excellence. In other words, even if nothing changes, tuition will have to go up by the amount identified as the base tuition gradient.

How do you decide what your base tuition gradient should be to support the strategic financial plan? Clearly, this number is intended to cover inflationary costs so that the value of the fees your school receives does not erode over time. However, the Consumer Price Index-Urban (CPI-U) does not completely reflect expenditures in private schools; it can only serve as a base figure. The base tuition gradient for private schools is inflation (adjusted for your local area) plus 2%. If you're happy with this explanation, you can skip the next, more technical, paragraphs and go on to the section on "Creating Your Strategic Financial Plan."

Technical Explanations

The following is provided for you (given the importance of the base tuition gradient concept for tuition setting) in case you really distrust this idea, or just want to understand it better.

The CPI has a built-in "productivity factor." It assumes the workforce is increasingly productive as computers, streamlined mechanical devices, and other laborsaving developments provide greater output with fewer personnel. The more efficient business becomes, the more inflation is stabilized or reduced.

Education differs from those kinds of industries in that it is people-intensive and not product-driven. Education cannot offset the total true effects of inflation by increased efficiency—the classroom still consists of a teacher and a group of students. If more students enroll, we create more sections with more teachers. Furthermore, even as the demand for additional programs (and teachers) occurs, schools tend not to remove any of the existing programs to lessen the budgetary crunch. Costs go up even when productivity remains static.

Baumol's Cost Disease

All service industries suffer from a phenomenon commonly called Baumol's cost disease. William Baumol, renowned economist at New York University, developed data that indicated costs in service-related businesses inherently rise faster than in product-oriented industries. This occurs because productivity in the labor-intensive service sector tends to lag behind manufacturing, and salaries in the service sector have to keep up with salaries in more productive industries. In short, the costs for health care, entertainment, insurance, law enforcement, and education will always rise faster than overall inflation.

More recently, economists Jack E. Triplett and Barry P. Bosworth reaffirmed Baumol's findings and inferences concerning productivity. They claim the problem comes in the "mismeasurement of output." How do you measure the productivity of a teacher, and thus quantify the salary cost? For tech-savvy teachers, computers can possibly improve productivity in the classroom. But labor-intensive industries (like education) have a limited ability to benefit from technological advances and inevitably experience higher real costs. The CPI can reflect the costs of producing automobiles or computers, but it is clearly a poor base for setting tuitions (which are largely determined by faculty compensation, your school's primary budget item).

Private schools must compete with other industries when attracting and retaining qualified employees—they must pay market-competitive salaries to maintain a mission-appropriate, skilled staff. If faculty compensation must rise at a greater rate than inflation, so must tuition.

The 2%+ Factor and Your Tuition

To increase productivity, each teacher would have to teach larger classes (unpopular with parents, students, and teachers) or teach more classes (unpopular with overworked faculty who may seek other employment if the load is too high). To maintain an equivalent operation, year to year, you need income that is at least 2% greater than the CPI to cover the additional hidden inflation. If your school does not keep one step ahead financially, quality will eventually be eroded through decreased faculty morale, diminished services, and deferred maintenance.

Creating Your Strategic Financial Plan

A sample 13-line strategic financial plan is shown on the next page, with an accompanying line-by-line explanation. Adapt this short document to your own situation. This allows all your Board members, financially savvy or not, to ground themselves confidently in the critical numbers they need to grasp to participate, as they must, in the (financial) life of the institution. Once your plan is in place, make sure that all Trustees become comfortable with these 13 lines and what they mean. Charge your Finance Committee and, especially, your Committee on Trustees with providing frequent, brief review sessions in your regular Board meetings so that every Board member stays current on the uses and implications of this heart-of-the-matter document. And the day that your financially "least comfortable" Trustee raises her or his hand and asks, "Yes ... but what will that new position do to Line 7 of our strategic financial plan? And what about Line 11?" your Board will have (financially) arrived!

Sample Strategic Financial Plan
Dollar figures in thousands (000s)

	Year 1	Year 2	Year 3	Year 4	Year 5	Year 6
1. Enrollment	200	200	200	200	200	200
2. Net tuition revenue	$1,000	$1,075	$1,156	$1,242	$1,335	$1,435
3. Other hard income	$50	$50	$50	$50	$50	$50
4. Total hard income	$1,050	$1,125	$1,206	$1,292	$1,385	$1,485
5. Operations expense	$1,167	$1,214	$1,262	$1,313	$1,365	$1,420
6. Hard income P&(L)	$(117)	$(89)	$(56)	$(21)	$20	$65
7. Hard income % coverage	90%	92.7%	95.6%	98.4%	101.5%	104.6%
8. Annual (noncapital) fundraising	$100	$100	$100	$100	$100	$100
9. Overall P&(L)	$(17)	$11	$44	$79	$120	$165
10. Annual to reserve funds	$0	$11	$44	$79	$88	$8
11. Total reserve funds	$0	$0	$38	$117	$205	$213
12. Annual to endowment (by policy)	$0	$0	$0	$0	$32	$157
13. Total endowment	$250	$250	$250	$250	$282	$439

This simple strategic financial plan shown above assumes:
- the school's cash position and zero reserve funds require rapid strategic reversal
- the reversal can be accomplished without the marketing-and-enrollment risks inherent in cutting programs, services, or positions; and
- enrollment can be stabilized at current levels (N=200)
- a 3.5%-per-year differential must be established between the expense gradient and the hard income gradient (in this case, 4% per year for the former and 7.5% per year for the latter). In this case, the 4%-per-year expense gradient is an estimate of inflationary increases only, a gradient ISM refers to as the "floor gradient." In this hypothetical school, all expenses, including salaries, will increase at an average of 4% during this plan to correct for the at-risk financial position the school currently occupies.

Strategic Financial Plan Explanation

Line 1: Enrollment. ISM encourages you to assume flat enrollment so that your projections will be as conservative as possible. Show enrollment increases only in circumstances in which (a) you have substantial waiting pools of mission-appropriate students at your entry point(s) and (b) you have adequate space available to add sections of students systematically throughout your grade configuration. Bear in mind that enrollment growth is solvency-positive only if you can handle the growth with current facilities and faculty and staff, i.e., if you are growing your enrollment only by filling "empty seats."

Line 2: Net tuition revenue. The dollar figure remaining after "unfunded tuition assistance" (not shown) is subtracted from "gross tuition revenue" (also not shown). As you read from Year 1 to Year 6, each number increases by 7.5%, the calculated tuition increase necessary for this school to move from its financially fragile position to one of real strength in six years.

Line 3: Other hard income. This includes monies other than tuition and fees that are "billed for" (such as profit from a summer sports program) or transferred internally (such as interest earned by your endowment). In this sample, about $12,000 of Line 3 is interest from the Line 13 endowment corpus of $250,000, while the other $38,000 is profit from summer programs.

Line 4: Total hard income. Total the previous two lines.

Line 5: Operations expense, including debt service. This line does not show noncash expenditures such as depreciation. As you read from Year 1 to Year 6, each number increases, the estimated inflationary increase necessary to keep the school "where it is" relative to inflation.

Line 6: Hard income P&(L). This projected year-end cash position as a loss (in parentheses) or profit, before adding solicited funds (i.e., monies generated by fundraising initiatives). See Line 8.

Line 7: Hard income % coverage. One of the major ISM Stability Markers, this is the percent of operations expense covered by hard income (i.e., monies that are "billed for" or that represent transferable interest from a cash corpus). As you read from Year 1 to Year 6, you see a progression from 90% coverage to well over 100% coverage, the mathematical result of setting the tuition gradient higher than the expense gradient. (The arithmetic: Divide Line 4 by Line 5.)

Line 8: Annual (noncapital) fundraising. This line shows all fundraising except capital campaign outcomes. The line is held constant for the same reason Lines 1 and 3 are held constant: so that the planners will be forced to make the numbers work without recourse to the "easy way(s) out." These might include (a) "We'll just show higher enrollment on Line 1," (b) "We'll just show bigger endowment yields on Line 3," or (c) "We'll just ask the Development Director to raise more money." Don't fall prey to these traps; not one of them can be relied on to fund your operations.

However, if you do, in fact, fill "empty seats" or earn more than expected endowment interest or raise more money than shown from your annual fund, that's wonderful. With this ISM-recommended approach, these increases (Lines 1, 3, or 8), studiously not assumed in your strategic financial plan, will simply cause you to run higher surpluses sooner. With these higher-than-assumed surpluses, you may choose to grow your reserves faster, accelerate your debt-reduction schedule, supplement your endowment growth, or move an item in your plan up a year because you have the hard-income-generated funds to do it sooner.

Line 9: Overall P&(L). This line shows your profit or loss (number in parentheses), year-by-year. It represents the sum of Lines 4 and 8 less Line 5.

Line 10: Annual to reserve funds. This is the amount of a given year's surplus (if any) applied to your cash reserve funds.

Line 11: Total reserve funds. As you read from Year 1 to Year 6, you see that, until Year 5, all surplus dollars (if any) are placed in the reserve fund(s). But in Years 5 and 6, less and less of the surplus goes to reserves because the plan has reached ISM's benchmark figure for funding reserves.

Note: The reason Line 11 shows zero in Year 2, despite a small surplus having been earned that year, is that the $17,000 deficit from Year 1—see Line 9—will be paid off before funding the reserve.

Line 12: Annual to endowment (by policy). This line shows the amount of surplus going to endowment, if any. Line 12 shows zero going to endowment in the first four years of the plan because reserves will be funded to the ISM benchmark before attending to endowment in this fashion.

Line 13: Total endowment. Line 13 projects no growth in the endowment because (a) usable interest is going to Line 3—other hard income—each year and (b) consistent with ISM's recommendations throughout the plan, conservative assumptions are used and investment success is not assumed. In Years 5 and 6, once the cash reserve is fully funded, surpluses are directed to grow the endowment.

Note: In a strategic plan and strategic financial plan, there are no unaccounted funds. The plan imposes a fiscal discipline that allows surplus funds to be directed ONLY to cash reserves, endowment, debt reduction, or strategic plan objectives.

Strategic Planning and Strategic Financial Planning Detours

You're preparing for strategic planning and strategic financial planning. As a Trustee, you take stock of the school's "state of the union" and note, with pride, aesthetic improvements in the physical plant, an exceptional spring musical, well-considered changes in the curriculum, schoolwide Science Olympiad participation, competitive Model United Nations teams, winning seasons for several athletic teams, a vibrant service learning program in all divisions, and other visible successes over the past several years.

You want to continue the favorable growth of your school and harness positive human energy during the upcoming strategic planning and strategic financial planning retreat. As you approach the planning session, however, don't allow the momentum of understandably favorable feelings to detour you and your fellow Trustees' process from a truly strategic path.

You might, for example, spend excessive time discussing these interesting and positive accomplishments—or give them undue priority when approving items for the plan. Such detours can result in a planning document that is too broad, unfocused, and nonstrategic to guide your Board and administration and, in general, to serve your school well in the coming years.

As a Trustee, make it your top priority to stay clearly focused on viability for the future. Is each item to be discussed "merely important" or actually strategic—i.e., specifically dedicated to enhancing the school's stability and solvency? Keep in mind that strategic planning culminates in a succinct, Board and School Head-created document. This plan identifies the prioritized strategic variables the school must address over six years to sustain (and strengthen) school's financial viability and its ability to deliver the school's mission.

ISM strongly encourages the financial prudence derived from:

— an accompanying strategic financial plan, which ensures the plan is rooted in reality by identifying the cost of achieving each of the goals; and

— the disciplined practice of planning to cover all new operations expenses with 100% hard income, i.e. tuition (irrespective of what current hard income coverage looks like).

Note: We believe that, even if you're not that interested in "financials," you must know and understand the strategic financial plan.

Detours can undermine these two important financial practices—or bypass them altogether. In preparing for and conducting your retreat, be particularly wary of these five kinds of detours, any of which can distract Boards from strategic focus.

Detour No. 1: Rely heavily on constituent opinion when identifying and prioritizing planning items

What constituents think matters, but not always in strategic planning. Board's often decide to survey specific constituent groups—students, parents, alumni, and teachers—which is fine for gathering opinions. However, proceed with caution! Use the responses only to further illustrate strategic needs, not determine them.

During your planning retreat, do not allow the survey results to constitute a detour. Your retreat is not the time to bask in constituent acknowledgment of top-rated areas, puzzle over unfavorable results, or seek specific corrective action by way of your plan. Use constituent opinion only if it has strategic implications as you craft and "vote for" planning items: publicizing next-level placement, enhancing internal marketing, or addressing student attrition at certain grade levels, for example.

You may be eager to seek "buy-in" for your plan among constituents and, as a result, over-focus on their participation and opinion before the retreat. Keep in mind that, in strategic planning and strategic financial planning, community support follows from the Board's success in marketing the planning document after it is written and approved. The strategic plan is the foundation and core referent for systematically fostering buy-in.

Detour No. 2: Emphasize student programs

When people think about school operations, it's the work of teachers and students that comes most readily to mind. Student programs—the math program, literacy, advising, athletics, clubs, and other activities—can attract significant interest and attention during strategic planning and strategic financial planning, creating a detour.

Why does it happen? You and your colleagues were students at one time (in one school or another), and many of you may be parents of current students. Add in the engaging quality of discussing student programs and Trustees' personal experiences. Everyone has a favorite cheerleading squad, the Senior Speech, the prom, winning the football championship, the choir tour, the Habitat for Humanity build! Additionally, you may be more familiar with public school Boards (and their oversight responsibilities) than with the strategic governance work of private school Boards. These factors can lead some Trustees to see themselves as "experts" in the programmatic work of schools and, even more destructive of strategic focus, see it as their job to plan and oversee that work.

Some components of student programs may, for a particular school, be strategic because they have an impact on the school's market niche (e.g., adding another academic program such as coding, or strengthening the advisory program). More often than not, though, these items are "merely important." As an antidote to the risk of this kind of detour, be sure that you receive (or provide) adequate education about truly strategic variables early in the planning retreat. Make sure everyone remembers that it is the role of the School Head to administer student programs and manage faculty.

Accumulating cash reserves or improving hard income coverage may not be "sexy" issues (both of these items are first tier Stability Markers). But they are likely to rank well ahead of student program changes as strategic matters for your plan.

Detour No. 3: Become preoccupied with what competitor schools are doing

As with constituent opinion, the external environment—the market in which your school operates—merits awareness. Do not, however, become distracted by trying to mimic what a competitor school across town is doing. Remember the strategic importance of re-recruiting current families by distinguishing the benefits students experience at your school and the value your parents receive for their tuition dollars. The strategic emphasis is internal: make your school strong and distinctive, and market these strengths and distinctions. (Note the importance placed on internal marketing at the top of the ISM X.) Too much external "scanning" can endanger the unique features of your school's particular mission and diminish the quality and amount of strategic attention to the school's institutional health.

Detour No. 4: Place excessive focus on capital items

Like student programs, new or renovated buildings or other large-scale capital improvements can create a detour. When these bricks-and-mortar items garner too much attention in both discussion and determination of items for the plan, other more abstract but strategic matters—such as Board structure and function, faculty culture, or a major gifts program—may be neglected.

It may be more interesting—and, in some ways, easier—to picture your school in the future by "seeing" buildings than it is to envision, for example:

- engendering and sustaining excellence in faculty through appropriate funding of daily immersion in growth and renewal;
- cultivating a major donors;
- identifying more effective ways for the Board to conduct its business.

It is, however, the Board's responsibility to be thoroughgoing in identifying the full range of strategic variables (ISM Stability Markers, in particular) that must be addressed in your plan. The "sizzle" and "busyness" of a capital campaign can obscure the real problems.

Attention to these strategic variables, in fact, is a prerequisite to achieve the kinds of fundraising goals that support capital projects. The more ambitious these projects, the more vital it is to have a planned and implemented strategic institutional infrastructure.

Detour No. 5: Ignore the cost and impact on tuition levels of noncapital planning items

Envisioning a school in the future can be exciting. Long-term, strategic purpose takes priority, however, over short-term enthusiasm. A strategic plan that lacks two components—the cost of the item and the source of revenue to cover that cost (including any impact on tuition)—becomes no more than a "wish list." Such a list often has a short shelf life. After the initial enthusiasm has faded, it provides little direction and clarity for creating yearly Board and administrative agendas, for setting (and marketing) tuition levels, and, ultimately, for fulfilling the school's vision across the life of the planning document.

Focus on the Future

As you move into strategic planning and strategic financial planning, keep the emphasis on components that move your school forward—and beware of detours. Supplement your planning document with a strategic financial plan and, as operations costs are envisioned, address the issue of increasing annual hard income in proportion to increased costs. From the Board's view, two attitudes will be critical in achieving decade long success.

- **Discipline:** This is a crucial characteristic for Boards that have strategic plans and strategic financial plans. The plan is not a guide—it is the thing itself. It is not written in stone, i.e., it can be changed annually and will be quadrennially. However, until the Board decides to change it, the plan is the only thing the Board can contemplate doing.

- **Patience:** The Board will hopefully be highly aspirational in its ambition for the children who do and who will attend the school. ISM sees no reason for those aspirations to unfulfilled over time. We have seen example after example of schools moving from achievement to achievement by being patiently aspirational. The Board's job is viability for the next generation—it and its successors had time to accomplish great things. Rarely need a Board be in a hurry.

A Strategic Plan-Strategic Financial Plan for an ISM Client School

Note: This plan, being "real," may not follow all the rules perfectly. This just means that in every school, including your own, there are particular circumstances that must be addressed. The principles, however, are always upheld.

Year One has no costs (and rarely will have any significant costs) since "this" year's budget has already been allocated. The most common exception to the rule is where an item is funded through cash reserves because of its immediate importance.

The base tuition gradient referenced in the text is the tuition increase required in any given year to (merely) maintain the current program at its current level of excellence. The measure of this is inflation plus 2%.

Beginning in Year Two, in the Costs column, the annotation $ refers to the percent of tuition increase required to permanently fund this item. Each $ refers to a 1% tuition increase over the base tuition gradient.

Note that not all strategic items have a cost attached to them. Often, an action may be one that is organizational or can be accomplished with volunteers (e.g., a Board committee).

Items are typically phased in over several years. The Board's orientation is that, over time, amazing things can be accomplished. Being in a hurry is not a virtue.

Year One			
Item	**New Costs**	**Revenue Source**	**Responsible Person or Entity**
1. Review the strategic plan annually. Create an annual agenda, derived from the strategic plan, and then charge Board committees to maximize effectiveness.	None	NA	Board
2. Use the Board self-assessment survey to enhance Board effectiveness. Administer survey annually.	None	NA	Board
3. Revisit the high school strategy and vision. Determine appropriate path forward and update strategy as necessary. Consider this within the scope of the current capital campaign and funds raised. Adjust the plan as necessary to build the K–12 school program.	TBD	Fundraising	Board/Admin
4. Endowment building—determine endowment goals and effective endowment campaign strategy in light of capital needs.	TBD	Fundraising	Board/Admin
5. Develop a plant and systems repair and replacement plan and funding strategy.	$200,000	Operations	Board/Admin

Year Two

Item	New Costs	Revenue Source	Responsible Person or Entity
1. Review and update as necessary our mission statement, Portrait of a Graduate, and Characteristics of Professional Excellence to clearly define the school's competitive difference.	None	NA	Board/Admin
2. Review and update our internal and external communications plan to assure timely and effective information to build our brand. We will evaluate the importance of Board communication to our constituents concerning major decisions and effective administrative communications.	None	NA	Board/Admin

Year Three

Item	New Costs	Revenue Source	Responsible Person or Entity
1. Partner with local university and develop a teacher training program.	None	NA	Admin
2. We remain committed to hire and retain outstanding faculty. We will continue to advance teacher compensation to attract and retain high-performing teachers.	$500,000	Operations	Admin
3. Hire an additional nurse and campus chaplain to support our student body.	$225,000	Operations	Admin
4. As the school continues to increase enrollment, add an Associate School Head to support curriculum development and to build the high school program.	$185,000	Operations	Admin

Year Four			
Item	**New Costs**	**Revenue Source**	**Responsible Person or Entity**
1. Using the current parent, student, and faculty surveys, review data and develop a communication plan about the results. Develop strategy and use data to enhance our program.	None	None	Admin
2. Develop a technology program for the entire school, primary through eighth grade. Consider skills necessary for high school. Expand technology as required.	$75,000	Operations	Admin
3. Enhance fine arts program. Include band, orchestra, and chorus.	$90,000	Operations	Admin

Your Strategic Financial Policy Document: A Sample

As you work with your strategic plan and strategic financial plan, a third component comes into play. Your strategic financial policy document is the verbal expression of the financial strategies and concepts that are layered into the strategic financial plan itself. These strategies and concepts are implicit in the financial plan—and, indeed, in the basic strategic plan. Your policy will clarify (in a concise, list-formatted statement of no more than three pages) the guiding principles that are operative in both plans.

This sample uses hypothetical concepts from our fictional coed, K–12 day school, Exempli Gratia Academy, and is derived from the imaginary school's freshly written strategic plan and strategic financial plan.

Introduction

The Board of Trustees of Exempli Gratia Academy, working with and through the School Head, employs a four-year cycle for the development of six-year strategic and strategic financial planning documents. (That is, the Board and Head develop six-year plans every four years.) The purpose of this policy statement is to list and describe the financial strategies and concepts that play through the most recent iteration of both strategic planning documents.

Strategies and Concepts

1. Hard income (i.e., operating revenues billed or transferred as earned interest from endowment) is to cover as high a percent of operations expense as possible, with 100% coverage as a theoretical—and, eventually, as an actual—goal.

2. Soft income (i.e., solicited funds) is to be generated, first, in support of "named enhancements" to the student programs; second, in support of small capital expenditures; and, finally, to the extent necessary, in support of the operations budget.

3. Undesignated operating surpluses are (generally) to be applied according to the following priorities: first, to accelerated debt reduction; second, to the build-up of cash reserves toward the ISM benchmark figure (see ISM Stability Marker No. 1 in Chapter Five); and third, to strengthening the endowment.

4. The floor gradient for use by the Board and School Head in the quadrennial strategic planning event shall be a number researched and recommended by the Board's Finance Committee. That number normally represents the best (i.e., most relevant) Consumer Price Index figure for your locale plus two percentage points. The two points are added to account for the CPI's under-prediction of inflation's impact on personnel-heavy operations budgets (such as those in schools), and operations which cannot, over time, increase their efficiency.

5. The published and publicized tuition gradient (the arithmetic outcome of the Board's most recent strategic planning event) is to be considered a commitment to the parent body. Annual tuition will not be allowed to exceed that published figure unless catastrophic events—weather-related, national or regional economy-related, or school enrollment-related—force such a change. In such an event, the normal expedient will be to create a fresh strategic plan and strategic financial plan and to communicate the new plan, and the rationale for creating it, to the parent body.

6. An annual financial audit will be conducted by a qualified accounting firm. The audit contract will be let out to bid at least once every four to five years. The Board's Finance Committee shall recommend an audit firm to the full Board on those occasions.

7. A line of credit shall be maintained in an amount equal to 10% of the overall operations budget. The interest rate on the LOC shall be renegotiated at least every 24 months by the Board's Finance Committee. (The line of credit is to be used for emergencies only; its normal balance should be zero.)

8. Employee benefits will be formally reviewed every 24 months by the Chief Financial Officer, and recommendations generated for consideration, first, by the Board's Finance Committee, and, second, by the full Board. If changes are undertaken, including a formal request for proposal (RFP), the new benefits package costs must conform to the existing strategic financial plan. If such changes cannot be accommodated by the current plan, then the changes must await development of the next scheduled strategic plan and strategic financial plan.

9. Repair and replacement of facilities or equipment shall be ongoing, supported normally by a budget line that shall contain an amount no less than 4% of the total operations budget.

10. The school shall maintain property and casualty, business interruption and extra expense, workers' compensation, and all forms of liability insurance limits sufficient to protect the school from losses of significant magnitude. The quadrennial strategic plan and strategic financial plan shall carry expenditure gradients adequate to cover these fundamental insurance responsibilities.

The sample shown above is not designed to be exhaustive, but suggestive of the kinds of items normally to be included in a strategic financial policy document. Obviously, the financial policy statement should be reviewed by the Finance Committee and the CFO at least as often as a new planning document is developed (i.e., every four years).

The Operating Budget

The school's operating budget is rooted in, but not the same as, the strategic financial plan. The strategic financial plan and the operating budget are complementary; they are independent processes that yield interdependent plans.

The strategic financial plan is a multiyear document and is considered at the highest strategic level. The operating budget is the day-to-day nuts and bolts and is derived as a result of the strategic plan.

The budget gives much greater detail than the strategic plan, and the budget lines are drilled into extensively. Creating the budget occurs annually, reflecting a single year. The starting point for creating the operating budget is the "total operating budget" line in the plan, corresponding to the current budget year. After that, the annual budgeting process takes on a life of its own. There are, of course, two sides of the operating budget—income and expenses. Ultimately, the outcome of the operating budget is to present a balanced budget, ensuring the school can continually fulfill the mission.

Expenses: Using the overall dollar goal determined by the strategic financial plan, the Business Manager and the Finance Committee usually will work closely with each Division Head within the school and each manager or leader. The goal is to understand each department's expense requirements for the upcoming year, testing the school's ability to operate within its fiscal realities. Once the Business Manager and the Finance Committee are confident that all the necessary expenses have been noted, it is time to work on the income side of the budget.

Income: Understanding income for independent schools is not complex. There are two basic types of revenue—hard and soft income. Soft income is money raised from the annual fund and fundraising events. Understanding the concept of the ratio of hard income coverage makes budgeting easy, and it connects the budget process to the strategic planning process, clarifying the relationship between the two interrelated documents. In simple terms, the hard income coverage ratio is all hard revenues divided by the total expense budget. This creates a percentage. The overall goal of good budgeting (and good strategic planning) is to keep the hard income coverage as close to 100% as possible. Therefore, once the expense requirements have been determined, the Business Manager calculates the tuition increase required to keep the hard income coverage ratio, at minimum, the same as the previous year's, or increases it if strategically appropriate.

Enrollment must be considered in understanding the revenue side of the operating budget. Working closely with the Admission Office, it is critical that the budget developers understand the anticipated enrollment outcomes. If enrollment is holding steady, there are few changes usually required in the operating budget. However, when enrollment increases or decreases, the budget formers have to make certain that operating costs are managed within income parameters.

Marketing Your Strategic Financial Plan

As with all things relating to strategic financial plans, the School Head (with the Board President's support) must market these documents to your parent body and other constituencies. For example, selected items in your financial policy might be highlighted, one or two at a time, in your newsletter, for communicating to the parent body:

(a) what the strategic financial policies actually are;

(b) how these policies play through the life of the school (e.g., in setting annual tuition levels); and

(c) how the Board of Trustees functions and what it concentrates on.

Many schools assemble the parent body in the auditorium, distribute a one-page summary of the new planning documents, and provide a punchy 30-minute overview of the expected outcomes (tiptoeing thoughtfully around the always-sensitive tuition implications of these plans).

If the school takes this approach, be prepared to deal with two major threats. One has to do with the essential nature of large groups; the other, with basic organizational courtesy, parent relations, and student retention.

Threat No. 1

A large-group setting is a dangerous format for presenting financial plans or plans that have obvious financial implications. Even one hostile and abrasive individual can turn this affair into a battleground in which few parents, if any, will be so courageous as to rally a defense.

Though you may have numerous allies or sympathizers in the audience, do not assume that they will be willing to engage the school contrarian in this highly public arena. As the frontline school leaders, the Head and the Board President will be left to fight this battle.

It won't make any difference how skillfully and courteously you handle the situation. In the end, unavoidably, the impression created will be that this is a school-vs.-parents contretemps in which your plans make sense only to the institution's leadership (i.e., senior administrators and the Board). Most in the audience are likely to feel vaguely unsettled regarding the efficacy of your planning documents.

Thus, just when you need your families to be most excited about the school's future, you have allowed a sense of foreboding to creep into their awareness. The cherished sense of community you have worked to build will have displayed its fragility in a highly public setting.

Threat No. 2

By "tiptoeing around" the tuition impact of your strategic plan and strategic financial plan, you do your parents a disservice and risk public relations damage.

Speak openly and plainly to parents about what the plans will mean to each of them in dollar terms. It is essential to give them the opportunity to do their own financial planning.

You also risk multiplying the public relations damage your adversaries may have already engendered simply by their questioning of the validity of your goals and the process you used to form them. Now they will also be able to emphasize (correctly) that you have sought to keep your constituents in the dark regarding what the plans will cost each of them.

How can you present your plan to the school community in a way that informs constituents, encourages support, and maintains stronger control over the outcome?

The Neighborhood Visit: Concept

Rather than bringing your families together in one large assembly, take your message and your excitement to them, on their turf, in small-group settings. True, this will be far more time- and labor-intensive for the School Head and the leadership. But you will, in the process, diminish the public relations risks, create a valuable opportunity to build and nurture relationships, and enhance the marketing impact of your plans many times over.

Yes, just as in the all-school situation, your contrarians will make an appearance in one or more of the small groups. The difference is: In groups of, say, 20 or fewer, those who are supportive of your plans, or even neutral (but fair-minded), will—and often with some enthusiasm—respond to your adversaries on your behalf.

In each of these presentations, disclose your financial plans in detail, including tuition and tuition-assistance gradients. Hide nothing from the participants, honoring each family member with the specifics of the school's future and the costs to them of reaching that future.

This organizational courtesy allows parents to do their own family financial planning in anticipation of the expected tuition (and tuition-assistance) gradients. This courtesy strengthens the school's relations with its parent body by virtue of "opening the future" to public inspection, thereby entrusting the contents of your top-level planning documents to your primary constituency.

This public inclusiveness also assists you with all aspects of community building, from parent relations and student retention to philanthropy. Emphasize that parents are part of the school family—the inner circle—by inviting them to understand the institutional future and by helping them to think about what they can expect for tuition and tuition assistance.

The latter should be at least as steep as the former. Look your parents in the eye and say, "We intend to lose no students for financial reasons as we put this strategic plan and strategic financial plan into place."

The Neighborhood Visit: Implementation

Each time you develop a fresh set of financial plans—or plans with financial implications—launch your neighborhood visits. As you make plans for meeting face-to-face with small groups of families on their turf, consider these guidelines.

- Invite every parent, in writing, to attend one of the neighborhood sessions. Do not require RSVPs; however, plan a follow-up call or email to ensure that parents received the invitation and reinforce the school's interest in having them attend. In the invitation, include:
  - the location of each meeting (preferably the good-sized living rooms of Board, staff, faculty members, or supportive parents in various geographical locations),
  - the date (weekday afternoons or evenings), and
  - the time (emphasize that the session will get under way punctually and end 75 minutes later).
- A three- or four-person team should represent the school at these meetings: the School Head, a Trustee, a teacher, and perhaps a staff member.
- While three of these four people can rotate on and off the team, the School Head must attend every session.
- The presenter in each session should be the person who communicates this kind of material most effectively to a small group (not necessarily the Head). Thus, the speaker's role may rotate among several people.
- Distribute a user-friendly summary of your strategic plan and strategic financial plan.
- Also have copies of the actual strategic plan and its strategic financial attachment available. Call parents' attention to the fact that you are providing them with complete information, and emphasize that they are welcome to take these more difficult-to-read internal documents with them as well.

- When your projected tuition gradient is presented, also include the tuition-assistance gradient, emphasizing that no student will have to leave the school for financial reasons.

While neighborhood visits are extraordinarily time-consuming for the Head, they surpass every other approach for communicating financially related information to parents. As a low-risk and effective way to build parent relations and (indirectly) student-body retention, these sessions are worth the time and effort they require.

Your Companion Annual Agendas

Your Board has completed the strategic planning and strategic financial planning process. It's now time to develop the annual Board agenda and the annual operations (or administrative) agenda. This approach is the most efficient means of implementing your strategic plan.

With this approach, the Board President and School Head meet toward the end of the school year to establish these two short, but critical, documents in preparation for the upcoming year. (In practice, the President's annual Board agenda is often set in May or June; the Head's annual operations agenda, in July or August. The exact timing is of little consequence.)

Imagine a situation in which your school is moving into Year Three of its strategic plan. Assume the following items appear in the Year Three listing. (Note that items with operations costs will have been "costed," and the tuition gradient set accordingly, during the original planning event.)

Year Three Strategic Plan
- Negotiate on purchase of contiguous property.
- Collect or generate financial and employee-benefits data in preparation for Year Four planning event.
- Collect or generate other pertinent data in preparation for Year Four planning event.
- Complete the "quiet phase" of the capital campaign; prepare for a "public phase" kick-off.
- Prepare (facilities, personnel, equipment, supplies) to expand to three sections (in first grade) in Year Four.
- Conduct search for new Year Four position of Facilities Manager.
- Initiate young-alumni (electronic) surveying system to gather data pertinent to success in executing the Purpose and Outcome Statements (see Chapter Six) developed in Year One.

The Board President selects from the Year Three list those items that are the Board's to implement; the School Head selects from the list those items that are the Leadership Team's to implement. The outcome of such partitioning with the example above might result in the following complementary agendas.

The Annual Board Agenda
- Complete negotiations on purchase of contiguous property.
- Collect or generate financial and employee-benefits data in preparation for the Year Four planning event.
- Collect or generate other pertinent data in preparation for the Year Four planning event.
- Complete the "quiet phase" of the capital campaign; prepare for a "public phase" kick-off.

The Annual Operations Agenda
- Prepare to expand to three sections (in first grade) in Year Four.
- Conduct search for new Year Four position of Facilities Manager.
- Initiate an online surveying system for alumni to gather data pertinent to the school's success in executing the Purpose and Outcome Statements developed in Year One.

Reminders

The Board President and Trustees must keep the following in mind.

- Your committee structure and your committee charges will need to reflect the tasks implicit in the annual Board agenda. For example, you may create a separate committee to "complete negotiations on purchase of contiguous property" (assuming that this has consisted only of informal conversations between school representatives—e.g., a Realtor on your Board and your Development Director—and the seller). For another example, charge the Finance Committee with:
    - an operations finance focus to concentrate on tracking the Year Three financials against your 13-line strategic financial plan; and
    - a strategic finance focus to devote time and energy to preparations for the Year Four planning event (e.g., preparing both a salary study and a benefits study).
- All of your committee charges must be written formally, with deadlines provided and enforced.

The School Head must keep the following in mind.

- Although strategic plan items Nos. 1, 3, and 4 (as well as No. 2) are listed as components in the annual Board agenda, you will play a critical role in the success of all three. (No. 2 is less likely to demand your engagement.)
- Firmly ground your Year Three Head evaluation criteria in the four items shown in the annual operations agenda and the three annual Board agenda items just noted (i.e., your support roles in the success of those three Board-level items comprise legitimate areas for evaluation).

Bear in mind the second-ranking ISM Stability Marker (see Chapter Five) is simply the existence and organizationally embedded use of a strategic plan and strategic financial plan meeting ISM's six criteria. The complementary agendas discussed in this chapter suggest why the plan itself ranks so high. Without the plan, both Board and operations agendas—when they are created at all—tend to "float," not necessarily related to the long-term, strategic success of your institution. With an ISM criteria-appropriate strategic plan in place, creation and implementation of the two annual agendas become fundamental to institution-wide strategic success.

The ISM Stability Markers

The ISM Stability Markers provide a research-based way to look at the strategic issues that Boards should consider to fulfill their trusteeship to the next generation of children. They provide metrics that are useful to the Board in determining the school's strategic direction. They do not speak to the current excellence of the school except as they determine a "today" position. Their use is in identifying areas that would be most powerful for the Board to improve as the school moves forward over the next four to six years.

The ISM Stability Markers comprise the best place to begin your strategic thinking. The Board's strategic role is contrasted with the School Head's operations role. The Board's job is to look after the next generation of students; the Head's job is to look after the current generation of students. It is rare indeed, and typically only in emergency situations, where this distinction is not maintained. Where overlaps occur, they occur within the committee framework (see Chapter Nine).

The Stability Markers Self-Scoring Instrument

ISM's suggested approach to self-scoring entails forming an ad hoc committee chaired by the Board President, School Head, or by an administrative designee. That committee includes at least one (other) Trustee, at least one teacher, the technology person, and the Business Manager. The committee divides the data-collection and data-generation tasks appropriately. For example, the Business Manager computes scores on the three Stability Markers that are explicitly financial. The technology professional determines which of the several surveys (of students, teachers, and Trustees) can be set up for electronic scoring. The Trustee communicates with the Board regarding the Board-specific survey.

Based on ISM's research, we have expanded the definition of excellence in executive leadership to include the School Head's level of flourishing across multiple aspects of psychological well-being. Stability Marker No. 3, Executive Leadership, is a measure of the School Head's leadership traits and points of emphasis that translate into his or her ability to lead a healthy faculty culture. The School Head's flourishing was found significantly to predict the health of the school's faculty culture. Therefore, we have added the School Head's self-rated level of flourishing to the total score for Stability Marker No. 3.

A major element is in the second-tier Stability Markers, dealing with the Board of Trustees structure and function. This involves weighted scoring for ISM's Strategic Board Assessment, a self-scoring instrument for use by Boards (see Chapter Thirteen).

A total of 147 points is possible. Judge your school's total against the four-category array ISM has recommended for some time.

- Category One (71 or fewer points). A self-score in this range suggests that, in strategic planning, the entire focus of the new plan should be on strengthening your school's scores on the Stability Markers.
- Category Two (72–101 points). A self-score in this range implies that your school has developed enough strategic strength to undertake a set of modest initiatives—i.e., moderate risks—while still protecting the core Stability Marker scores already achieved.
- Category Three (102–131 points). A self-score in this range implies that your school has developed enough strategic strength to undertake constituency-based planning, if your situation calls for that. There are risks inherent to gathering large numbers of your constituents and asking

them to help construct a vision for your school's future. Unless you have a strategic financial framework in place to act as a constraint on the ideas that will be generated, you risk developing a plan you cannot afford. Nonetheless, if carefully planned and controlled, constituency-based planning can develop strong community support for your new plan.

- Category Four (132–147 points). A self-score in this range indicates your school has achieved an enviable stability level. It can afford to undertake constituency-based planning without fear that the additional expense layered into your new plan will be likely to weaken the school and cause it to regress toward lower Stability Marker categories. This does not mean, of course, the new plan should be financially reckless. It should guard its current high-scored Stability Markers just as judiciously as a Category-One school.

ISM Stability Markers Scoring Instrument

Section A: First-Tier Items (Rank-ordered)

Stability Marker No. 1: Cash Reserves, Debt, and Endowment Mix

A. Sum all cash reserves—monies that can be accessed by Board vote, as distinct from true endowment, which cannot—and express as a percent of operating expenditures. Make these and all financial calculations based on a cash translation of your operating budget (e.g., expenses include interest and principal on loans, but do not include depreciation when depreciation is a "paper number").

 Award points on a 0–15 scale, as follows:

   20%+ = 15 points

   15%–19% = 12 points

   10%–14% = 9 points

   5%–9% = 6 points

   3%–4% = 3 points

B. Compute the market value of your endowment fund balance. Divide that balance by total debt to achieve a ratio. In situations in which there is none of either, award the midrange score of 7.5).

 Award points on a 0–15 scale, as follows:

   10 to 1 or higher = 15 points

   5–9 to 1 = 12 points

   3–4 to 1 = 9 points

   2 to 1 = 6 points

   1 to 1 = 3 points

C. Ascertain annual debt service on outstanding obligations (interest and principal on debts). Express as a percent of operating expenditures (not operating revenues). Award points on a 0–15 scale, as follows:

   0% to 0.9% = 15 points

   1% to 1.9% = 12 points

   2% to 2.9% = 9 points

   3% to 3.9% = 6 points

   4% to 5.9% = 3 points

D. Average the scores for B and C (to yield BC).

E. Average A with BC.

Enter E (range of 0–15 points): _____

Stability Marker No. 2: Strategic Plan and Strategic Financial Plan (incorporating an updated risk-management plan) and Strategic-Plan-Based Budgeting

Scoring is "all or nothing." Award 12 points if you have a plan that:

a. extends at least four years into the future (from time of development);

b. deals primarily with viability-related items (those dealing with money, organizational structure, technology, facilities and grounds, and general positioning in the marketplace);

c. deals with the financial and quantitative consequences of those items;

d. displays the projected net tuition gradient and other hard-income gradients;

e. displays the basic expense gradient;

f. includes an updated risk-management plan;

g. is in routine (at least monthly) use by the Board and administrative leadership; and

h. invites the administration and Finance Committee to build the annual budget around the resulting planning document.

Award 12 points (0 or 12): _____

Stability Marker No. 3: Executive Leadership

Using the ISM Executive Leadership Survey (see the Appendices), set the items into a four-point scale and distribute the 20-item survey to all faculty members. With the results in hand, award 1 point for each instance in which at least 75% of the respondents selected the 3 or the 4 (i.e., the "good end of the scale"). Sum the 75%-plus items and multiply that result by 0.4 to earn a maximum of 8 points.

Using the eight-Item Diener Flourishing Scale, invite the School Head to rate him or herself using the seven-point scale. Sum the total and divide by 14.

Add two scores and enter the result (0–12 range): _____

Stability Marker No. 4: Hard-Income Driven

Determine the total amount of hard income in the operations budget. This refers to monies that are billed—for example, tuition, fees, summer-program income, income from facilities rental, bookstore sales—and to usable interest generated from interest-bearing accounts, such as endowment. (Use net tuition revenue for this purpose, i.e., gross tuition revenue minus your "unfunded tuition assistance" —your discounts—in all categories.) Divide that number by total operations expenditures, including debt service (principal and interest) but not "paper numbers" such as depreciation.

Award points for day schools as follows:

> 100%+ = 12 points
> 95%–99.9% = 9 points
> 93.5%–94.9% = 6 points
> 92%–93.4% = 3 points

Award points for boarding schools as follows:

> 80%+ = 12 points
> 78%–79.9% = 9 points
> 76%–77.9% = 6 points
> 74%–75.9% = 3 points

Enter the result (0–12 range): _____

Stability Marker No. 5: The Faculty Culture and the Student Experience

This item is scored by administering ISM's Faculty Culture Profile (see Appendices) and Student Experience Profile (see also Appendices) to all students in grades 5–12, and converting the two scores into a 12-point summary score.

For the Faculty Culture Profile, award one point for each instance in which at least 75% of the respondents selected the 7, 8, or 9 on the nine-point scale. Multiply your final result on the Faculty Culture Profile by 0.3 to convert to a six-point scale.

For the Student Experience Profile, award one point for each instance in which at least 51% of the respondents selected the 7, 8, or 9 on the nine-point scale. Multiply the outcome by 0.5 to convert the outcome to a six-point scale.

(Note: When scoring the Student Experience Profile for any purpose other than awarding Stability Marker points, a completely different approach is used, resulting in a score for each of this instrument's three scales: Predictability and Support, Student Satisfaction, and Student Enthusiasm.)

Sum the two six-point (maximum) outcomes and enter (0–12 scale): _____

Stability Marker No. 6: Enrollment Demand in Excess of Supply

Award as many as 6 points for a track record over the last three years, continuing through today, of a substantial waiting pool of mission-appropriate students (with appropriate balance between full-pay and partial-pay) wishing to enroll at your school's major entry point or points. Award 0–6 points.

Next, determine your retention (re-recruitment) rate based on your track record over the last three years; award 6 points for an overall figure of 90% or greater. This part of Stability Marker No. 6 scoring is "all or nothing": award 6 points or 0.

Record your estimate (0–12 range): _____

Subtotal for Section A (First-Tier Items, range 0–75): _____

Section B: Second-Tier Items (Not rank-ordered)

Stability Marker A: The Strategic Board

See the ISM survey instrument titled Strategic Board Assessment. Administer the survey to all Trustees. Follow the scoring instructions shown as part of the instrument.

Enter the result (0–24 range): _____

Stability Marker B: Consistent Donor Engagement

Score this item by considering to what extent your school fully and appropriately attends to your donors and prospects throughout the six stages of the Donor Cycle:

    a. identify,

    b. engage,

    c. evaluate,

    d. solicit,

e. recognize, and

f. steward.

Award up to 1 point for consistently high performance on each of the six stages.

Enter the result (0–6 range): _____

Stability Marker C: Development Office Management

Score this item by assessing the Development Office's ability to:

a. collect, organize, and analyze financial and other data;

b. provide direct and logistical support for all stages of the Donor Cycle; and

c. provide data and analysis as needed to support school operations and governance.

Award 0 to 2 points for performance in each of these three areas.

Enter the result (0–6 range): _____

Stability Marker D: Internal Marketing

Award up to 1.5 points for each of the following, up to a total of 6 points, for the existence of an Enrollment Management Team (by any name):

a. that is made up of key administrators from all areas of the school (e.g., admission, marketing communications, development, finance, Division Heads, school counselors, others);

b. that regularly collects and reviews data (e.g., constituent satisfaction, enrollment, school culture);

c. that uses data to develop a schoolwide enrollment management plan; and

d. that engages the faculty systematically in all internal marketing and re-recruitment efforts.

Enter the result (0–6 range): _____

Stability Marker E: Faculty Salaries

Determine the faculty's consensus referent (e.g., local public school median, regional association data, national association data). Rate your school's salary structure (median, mean, low-end, high-end) against the consensus referent, using a six-point "competitiveness" lens to decide on your estimate. (Example: With a public school median salary of $75,000, award 6 points tentatively if your own faculty median is equal to, or higher than, that figure; 5 points tentatively if within three percentage points of that figure; 4 points tentatively if within six percentage points of that figure; and so on. The word "tentatively" is to suggest that the median-to-median relationship comprises only a portion of your estimate—low-end and high-end salaries must also be considered. The final estimate will necessarily be subjective.)

Record your estimate (0–6 range): _____

Stability Marker F: Employee Benefits

Unlike the previous item, this is not a comparative or competitive Stability Marker. Rather, this Marker refers to the breadth of offerings in your school's benefit package. A sample list might include life insurance, health insurance, retirement plan, long-term disability, short-term disability, long-term care, dental insurance, vision insurance, employee assistance services, Flexible Spending Accounts. Using a six-point lens, subjectively determine your school's rating, with the inclusion of six or more of the above being likely to justify the awarding of all 6 available points, three justifying 3 points, and one justifying 1 point.

Record your estimate (0–6 range): _____

Stability Marker G: Budgeted Support for Faculty Professional Development

Determine from your operations budget the amount of funding allocated to faculty professional development. Express that number as a percent of total expenditures (ISM benchmark 2.0%). Multiply that percentage by 3.0 to convert to a six-point scale. (Note the ceiling is 6 points.)

Enter the result (0–6): _____

Stability Marker H: Quality of Facilities

Using "facilitation of the delivery of the school mission" as your lens, estimate your facilities' impact on the overall teaching and learning health of the physical environment. Consider the issue from all community viewpoints: student, teacher, coach, administrator, and parent. Consider all aspects of your facilities: classroom design and classroom space, storage space, music and art spaces, technological adequacy, athletics spaces (indoor and outdoor), administrative spaces, "great room" spaces, other assembly areas, and worship spaces in schools with religious missions. Award 6 points for facilities that are judged to enhance mission delivery across the board, and 0 for facilities that actually interfere with mission delivery.

Record your estimate (0–6 range): _____

Stability Marker I: Master Property, Facilities, and Technological-Infrastructure Plan

Subjectively award 6 points for plan(s) that include

a. a facilities audit;

b. a Campus Master Development Plan;

c. a Land Acquisition Plan; and

d. a Technological-Infrastructure Plan, with projected revenue sources for each one.

Award (up to) 1.5 points for each.

Record your estimate (0–6 range): _____

Subtotal for Section B (Second-Tier Items, range 0–72): _____

Add Subtotal for Section A (First-Tier Items, range 0–75): _____

Total Score (range 0–147): _____

The scoring instrument for Stability Marker No. 3 involves the ISM Executive Leadership Survey (see Appendices), which includes 20 statements set up on a four-point scale.

Our School Head:

1. vigorously seeks a professional growth and development-focused faculty culture;

2. gives public, positive reinforcement to deserving employees in all categories—especially in regard to laudable professional growth and achievements—and to students at all levels;

3. actively promotes an ongoing faculty conversation about high expectations and support for students;

4. seeks to establish a faculty-wide conversation about professional development;

5. places great emphasis on the faculty's specific-to-each-student high expectations;
6. demonstrates an inspired and inspirational commitment to the institutional mission;
7. sustains a high level of self-knowledge, self-awareness, and self-management;
8. exhibits determined pursuit of her or his own professional growth program;
9. is respectful of others, regardless of their position in the organization;
10. is a charismatic person;
11. displays great flexibility;
12. is a supportive person;
13. is steeped in moral purpose, moral clarity, moral conviction, and integrity;
14. is a highly ethical person;
15. is predictable. One can rely on the consistency of her or his responses to events, both "good" and "bad";
16. does not seem self-righteous;
17. tries to be supportive all the time and with everyone, regardless of their successes or failures (i.e., gives support even when it may not be merited);
18. shows respect for others in her or his formal interactions, such as presiding over meetings.
19. is a contemplative person; and
20. allows her or his humility to enhance her or his leadership.

The ISM X

The purpose of the ISM X™ is to assist strategic planners—Board members and senior administrators—in understanding how the ISM Stability Markers relate to each other. The graphic centrality of the Strategic Board, and the vertical ascent from Strategic Board through the Strategic Plan/Strategic Financial Plan through Executive Leadership and up to Student Demand/Enrollment, combine to highlight the several core variables comprising institutional sustainability. The starting point is—always—your Board's willingness to operate strategically and to plan strategically. Without these, the structure will be forever unstable.

The base of the ISM X is graphically dominated by the Strategic Board rectangle, centered in the bottom row of the base of the X. The Strategic Board—the outcome of the Board's self-score on the Strategic Board Assessment—is now Stability Marker Letter A, the first-listed second-tier Stability Marker in the fifth iteration. Placed directly above the Strategic Board, at the base of the revised ISM X, is the acronym "SP/SFP," representing your Strategic Plan and Strategic Financial Plan (ISM Stability Marker No. 2, the second-ranked Stability Marker in the fifth iteration).

The heavy black arrow pointing up from the center of the base of the ISM X leads to the Executive Leadership circle (ISM Stability Marker No. 3) and continues up to the three Stability Markers at the top of the ISM X: Internal Marketing, Healthy School Culture, and Student Demand/Enrollment. These elements, comprising the center and top of the X, are graphically unchanged from the fourth iteration, although scoring on all ISM Stability Markers is under continuous modification to reflect incoming data.

Along the base of the X, the eight Stability Markers flanking the Strategic Board and the SP/SFP acronym are unchanged (aside from continuous scoring modifications) except for their positioning. They are grouped more coherently than before, now reading from left to right on the second row from the bottom—Faculty Professional Development (funding); Faculty Salaries; Employee Benefits; Quality of Facilities; Development Office Management; and Donor Engagement. On the bottom row, there are now the Master Infrastructure Plan, on the left, and the Percent Coverage of Operations Expense With Hard Income, on the right.

Finally, at the extreme lower right, the ISM X shows Stability Marker No. 1, a formulaic mix of Cash Reserves, Endowment, Debt, and Annual Debt Service (principal and interest). Its positioning below the base of the X is designed to communicate that Stability Marker No. 1 is an outcome of high-level institutional performance throughout the ISM X, just as is Student Demand/Enrollment, also shown as an outcome, but in the extreme upper right of the display.

Stability Marker Fatigue: The Cure

While some Boards may be relatively new to these variables and their planning implications, many others may be experiencing factors that may contribute to the Stability Markers being undervalued or even dismissed. The outcome of these factors over time is "Stability Marker fatigue," a chronic condition that can usurp Board culture and contribute to institutional health problems down the road.

The ISM X

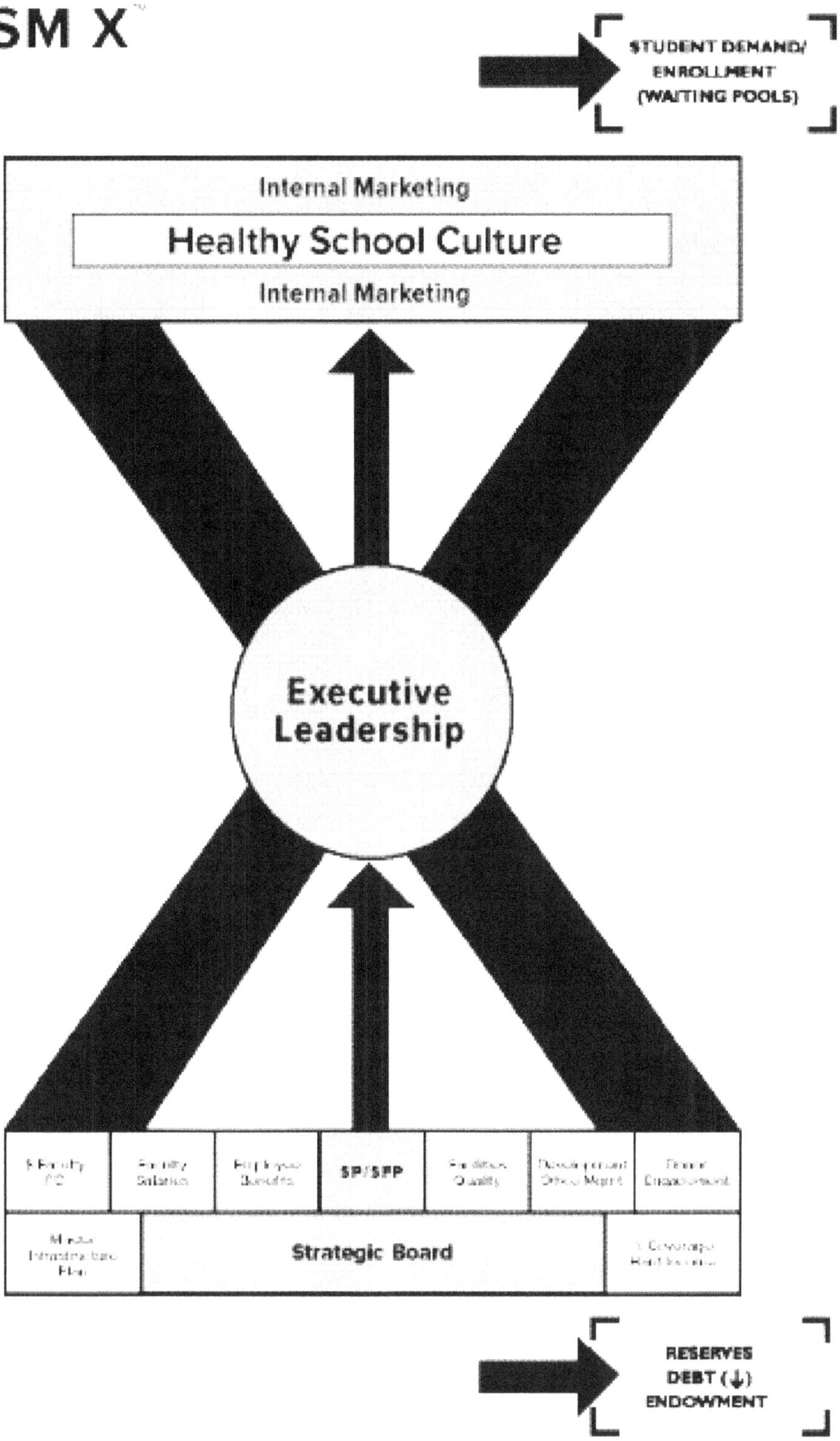

What Causes the Fatigue?

First, the Stability Markers are not "sexy"—they do not have the human appeal that, for example, curriculum, athletics, and other cocurricular activities or new buildings typically have. It is admittedly more emotionally engaging for adults (Trustees) to envision what students will be doing (academic work, sports, arts) and where they will be doing it (classrooms, computer labs, playing fields) than, for example, monitoring the annual increase in the percentage of hard-income coverage of operations expense.

Second, while some markers are articulated with quantified benchmarks (e.g., defined percentage to target for cash reserves), others are measurable only by surveys or even less precise methods. In these cases, interest in monitoring over time may fade.

Third, sometimes Boards become overfocused on constituent opinion. They allow the processes of seeking that opinion and then debating appropriate responses to dominate the agenda.

Finally, Board composition changes each year, and new Trustees may bring in "new ideas" with an energy that may redirect fatigued Trustees' attention (e.g., building a football stadium rather than solidifying the major gifts program).

The Antidote

Boards stray from their fundamental strategic purpose if they fail to keep in mind that the Stability Markers are not end points to be attained, but indicators of institutional health to be sustained. ISM has encouraged Boards to acquire and demonstrate several strategic, behavioral characteristics: objectivity, due diligence, and vigilance, among others. It is your Board's obligation to make judgments and take action for both attaining and sustaining institutional health by exercising a daily dose of the three Ds: **dedication, diligence,** and **discipline.**

The best way to ensure institutional health and to enhance the robustness of your Board's three Ds is to focus on two major structures—your strategic financial plan and your strategic Board committees. The former establishes key assumptions and financial parameters as ongoing (and moving) targets expressed in the annual operating budget. The latter, with the oversight of the Committee on Trustees, ensures that specific—and ongoing—action (delineated in committee charges) is being taken on behalf of strategic goals as defined by the Stability Markers and, ideally, as articulated in your current planning document.

A Board that aspires to enhance strategic functioning would do well to consider Stability Markers as a constant work in progress. A school cannot ever be "done" with markers of health. Attaining and maintaining "good (or excellent) shape," as defined by the best available markers of it, directly contribute to a long and healthy life for your school and the generations of students it will serve.

CHAPTER SIX

Purpose and Outcome Statements

While a mission statement is valuable, no matter how beautiful the wording, it is frequently inadequate. Many mission statements are considered unsatisfactory by the faculty and staff, the administration, the parent body, and others with an interest in the school (e.g., alumni, prospective donors).

A mission statement may fail to capture the essence of a school or provide any clear distinction from other schools. It may not be definitive enough to provide guidance to the Board, administration, or faculty in their pursuit of programmatic excellence. It may not answer the essential question, "Why does our school exist?"

Is it possible for a mission statement alone to accomplish the tasks of capturing the core reasons for your school's existence, distinguishing it from all others, and guiding your school in achieving its educational purposes? ISM's answer is, "No, probably not. It is, however, a beginning."

With the mission statement, schools should have two other definitive documents that guide the school in addressing the three above concerns. ISM calls this group of documents Purpose and Outcome Statements. To a short (no more than 30-word) mission statement, add:

– a Portrait of the Graduate (a list of desired student outcomes) and

– Characteristics of Professional Excellence (a list of characteristics serving as an operational definition of your faculty ideal).

The action element that energizes and provides a foundation for these statements is a strategic plan and complementary strategic financial plan. The strategic plan dictates your school's near-term future, and the financial plan serves as the "fuel" to enable its completion.

Your School's Mission Statement

One or more of these documents may exist in your school. Surely, there is a mission statement. There may also be a strategic plan and strategic financial plan and one or both of the others. The question is whether the existing statements provide the scope and guidance your school needs to define its purposes and outcomes in a directive, clear, and distinguishing manner.

Restating Your Mission

If your mission statement fails to meet these just-listed criteria or is just too "soft," consider an exercise to upgrade the statement. This can be a task for members of the Board, the Leadership Team, the faculty, or a combination of these appropriate people. However restating the mission is addressed, the final version must be formally adopted by the Board.

- Provide a definition for a mission statement such as the following: "Our school's mission statement is a 30-word (or fewer) declaration of our essential purpose as an institution. It is not comprehensive. It is value-laden. It differentiates our school from its competitors. It is memorable and marketable."

- Review this sample mission statement, examining the core words and phrases: "Our school's mission is to prepare students, in a diverse and nurturing environment, for next-level academic success, and to develop fully their individual ethical, social, physical, and spiritual capacities." The core phrases include "next-level," "academic success," "diverse environment," "ethical development," "social development," "physical development," and "spiritual development."

- Now, look closely at your own mission statement's words and phrases. Discuss the extent to which they meet the definition suggested in the first bullet point. The statement:

    a) is 30 words or fewer,

    b) summarizes your essential purpose,

    c) is not comprehensive,

    d) expresses your values,

    e) differentiates your school from its competitors, and

    f) is "memorizable." (In the example in the second bullet point, the statement clearly succeeds on "a," may or may not succeed on "b" and "f," and arguably fails on all the rest.)

- Ask, "Why does our school exist?" Brainstorm answers that describe those qualities your school values as an educational institution. Once all descriptors have been elicited, prioritize the top four or five value-laden reasons for your school's existence.

- Bring the mission restating exercise to a close. Assign the next step(s) to a small committee whose members have agreed, before the meeting, to serve. This committee's task will be to restate the mission to fit the criteria listed in bullet points one and three. Give a deadline (six weeks) to deliver the final version. Make it clear that a final version will then be presented to the Board for approval and adoption.

While you may choose to make mission restatement the first step in developing your school's Purpose and Outcome Statements, there is no prescribed order. You can create or revise either of the others (Portrait of the Graduate and Characteristics of Professional Excellence) first.

An Exercise in Restating a Mission

Here is an example of a restated mission developed by Exempli Gratia Academy after following this process. The result of the brainstorming and prioritization exercise yielded the following high-priority, value-laden reasons why the school exists.

- Knowledge empowers people
- Skills enhance lives
- Learning stimulates growth
- Ethical living brings dignity

The committee developed the following mission:

Exempl Gratia Academy empowers students by enhancing their lives, stimulating intellectual growth, instilling moral and ethical precepts, and fostering the dignity of each student.

Portrait of the Graduate

The Portrait of the Graduate is a list of five or fewer items comprising short descriptors of your "product"—the student developed over the years that she or he has spent under your faculty's tutelage. Examples of such descriptors may include:

- ready to perform with distinction at the next academic level;
- committed to lifelong learning, both inside and outside educational (institutional) contexts;
- conversant with the ethical implications of the school mission statement;
- competent in the use of technological research channels;
- committed to advancing the fine arts;
- eager to engage diverse communities;
- committed to community service principles; and
- able to articulate the major ingredients in a lifelong wellness lifestyle.

Schools with explicitly religious missions will include appropriate descriptors in their portraits, such as:

- committed to a biblically focused lifestyle;
- able to articulate fully the personal and ethical implications of a lifelong faith commitment; and
- tolerant of, and conversant with, other religious viewpoints.

Keep your Portrait of the Graduate concise. The impact of your portrait on readers diminishes as the list grows.

Developing Your Portrait of the Graduate

The School Head initiates developing your Portrait of the Graduate. Determination of the exact steps and selection of individuals to participate in the process will be the Head's choice. To spearhead the process, the Head forms a team, certainly to include teachers. (There may be a pre-existing group to assign the task, e.g., a "design team" of teachers who routinely provide advice and counsel to you. Perhaps assemble a mixed group with teachers, administrators, and others who regularly take on projects of this sort. Or there could be a standing administrative committee to which you could add appropriate faculty representation.)

Future Use of Your Portrait of the Graduate

Once your Portrait of the Graduate is in place, revisit it in during your quadrennial strategic planning events. Your portrait can be "tweaked" routinely without the kinds of ripple effects (through your community, your alumni, your accreditation agency, et. al.) that ensue inevitably with alterations to your mission statement. Use the portrait to emphasize your school's uniqueness and continue to differentiate yourself within your competitive marketplace.

Characteristics of Professional Excellence

The third component of your Purpose and Outcome Statements is your list of Characteristics of Professional Excellence. This is a 10- to 15-item list comprising your operational definition of faculty excellence. The items will relate both to your mission statement and to your Portrait of the Graduate. But they differ because they focus on the specific behaviors, values, and attitudes that must be present in strength within your faculty for the mission to come alive and the portrait to be realized.

Characteristics of Professional Excellence may include:

- knowledge of "innovative" content and process;
- high—but not uniform—standards for and expectations of all students;
- high time-on-action tasks for all students;
- explicit test preparation for all graded (i.e., evaluated) events;
- mission-consistent discipline in all instances;
- meaningful emotional and psychological engagement with all students;
- active support for colleagues;
- positive contribution to professional, mission-focused "sense of community" with all constituent groups;
- responsiveness to student needs; and
- responsiveness to parent needs.

Schools with religious missions may, of course, include explicitly religious descriptors in their Characteristics of Professional Excellence, such as:

- serving as a mature role model for a biblically focused lifestyle;
- displaying a seasoned capacity to articulate the personal and ethical implications of a lifelong faith commitment; and
- embodying proper public and private tolerance of, and respect for, other religious points of view.

Emphasize the importance of including items that are "difference-makers" in developing and preserving your faculty culture. Expect, for the sake of clarity, to develop a companion list of two-sentence explanations and examples for each item. This reduces the potential for misinterpretation—inadvertent or not—in your teachers individually consider the meaning of each of the items.

Development of Your School's Characteristics of Professional Excellence

As with the Portrait of the Graduate, the School Head starts developing the Characteristics of Professional Excellence. While the Head decides about the exact process and about the participants in that process, there is a general set of guidelines.

The Head should select a team to spearhead to develop the Excellence Characteristics, bearing in mind two factors. (1) Faculty participation is essential. These descriptors define the essence of "professionalism" in your school. (2) Academic administrative participation may be essential as well, since a parallel use of the Excellence Characteristics will be in the context of faculty evaluation. Academic administrators must consider these characteristics from a teacher-evaluation perspective and a definition-of-professionalism perspective.

Create or identify a single group—not a group for each academic division—to compile this list. These Excellence Characteristics, once formulated, operationally define what it means to be an exemplary professional faculty member in your school. Do not allow this definition to be fragmented by division.

Once complete, use your list of Excellence Characteristics:

- to combine with your mission statement and your Portrait of the Graduate to form a three-part foundation for all internal and external marketing efforts; and
- to be incorporated into your faculty evaluation system.

Revisit the Excellence Characteristics with your quadrennial strategic planning events or re-accreditation process. Routinely adjust your list to conform to your teachers' and your administrators' life experiences with the items.

ISM Success Predictors

Boards and senior administrators use the Stability Markers as a lens for self-evaluation and as a vector on which to move to strengthen a school's longest-term financial and organizational stability and excellence.

The ISM Success Predictors—not to be confused with the Stability Markers—represent ISM's deliberately considered speculation on what will be needed in private schools as they adjust to the always-changing technological, educational, and cultural milieu in which they move. The ISM Success Predicators, unlike the ISM Stability Markers, are not evidence-driven in the same way, i.e., not as outcomes of data analysis. Readers should understand the ISM Success Predictors are forecasts—not conclusions from data—of what ISM expects to be needed to achieve long-term success in the private school marketplace.

The ISM Stability Markers do not in any sense lose their utility as an evidence-driven set of benchmarks. However, the ISM Stability Markers' point of departure is by necessity private schools as we have known them in the past and present, not necessarily as we will know them in the future. Thus, the ISM Success Predictors are offered not as replacements for the ISM Stability Markers, but as supplements to them. This Success Predictor array can be expected to influence private schools' actual operations going forward, eventually to contribute to changes in ISM's data-driven list of Stability Markers.

The ISM Success Predictors do not comprise ISM's predictions of what will happen, but, rather, ISM's predictions of what will become necessary to establish and sustain institutional success.

The Success Predictors shown following are organized into (a) three Meta-Success Predictors and (b) 10 Correlative Success Predictors. The Meta-Predictors comprise large, organizationally complex ideas and actions that, singly and in combination with each other, will influence profoundly school leaders' decisions regarding the 10 Correlative Predictors that follow them.

Three Meta-Predictors

1. **Alignment and validation of Purposes and Outcomes with operations and resources.** Advancement programming (marketing communications, admission and enrollment management, development, and constituent relations) designed to reinforce the concept of school community-as-affinity-group.

    Examples:
    - creation, dissemination, and continual reinforcement to all constituent groups, internal and external, of a polished set of Purpose and Outcome Statements. This may include a short, evocative school mission statement coupled with a brief, high-impact Portrait of the Graduate (containing no more than four three-to-eight-word predicates) and, separately, a set of Characteristics of Professional (Faculty) Excellence. The latter serves as a lens through which to focus faculty and staff capacity to excel in the developing teaching, advising, and learning paradigm (see Meta-Predictor No. 2 following);
    - portrayal of students-as-brand, e.g., use of the web home page as a platform for display of the Purpose and Outcome Statements. This may feature only the P&O Statements and a montage of students in P&O-specific action, highlighting the school "brand" with students shown working and playing in ways not likely to be seen at that school;
    - use of ISM's Predictability and Support concepts as unifying themes—as

distinct from particular teaching or management or parenting methods—in:

1) faculty and staff professional development;

2) enhancement of faculty-advancement-finance staff interrelationships;

3) parent education (regarding the school's instructional focus); and

4) parenting education (regarding predictable and supportive parental roles at home);

– nurturing of collaborative interrelationships throughout the school community to the end that the school serves as a major affinity group, a center for purposeful, constructive communication and mutual support;

– development of internal and external marketing themes that consistently highlight the school's core differentiators: the constellation of student programs and experiences that are not replicated locally.

2. **Faculty and staff professional development.** Year-round investment in developing mastery-based, tech-supported, customized teaching, advising, and learning.

Examples:

– movement to 39–48-week faculty and staff calendars, with the equivalent of three-to-six weeks without students (but at full salary). Allocate those weeks solely to professional development practices that focus on mastery-based, tech-supported, customized teaching, advising, and learning;

– use of a faculty development system as the framework within which to address mission-focused teacher hiring, induction, evaluation, and professional growth (which focus on mastery-based, tech-supported, customized teaching, advising, and learning). Further, see (above) Meta-Predictor No. 1, letters a, b, and c, for discussion of the integration of ISM's Purpose and Outcome Statement concepts into all aspects of Meta-Predictor No. 2;

– continual focus on, and enhancement of, student well-being through policies, the schedule, and advisory programs. These explicitly support the just-listed curricular and instructional emphasis on mastery-based, tech-supported, customized teaching, advising, and learning. In the process, they link the predictability and supportiveness in the academic and cocurricular programs to predictability and supportiveness in the preparation-for-life themes implicit in the concept of school-community-as-affinity-group (see again, Meta-Predictor No. 1, above).

3. **Schedule.** Comprehensive student, faculty, staff, parent, and community schedules focused on making Meta-Predictors No. 1 and No. 2 symbiotic, both from a daily organizational and from an annual calendar standpoint.

   Examples:

   – creation of an annual calendar or schedule that gives primacy to mastery-based, tech-supported, customized teaching, advising, and learning for each individual student;

   – creation of an annual calendar that, having addressed letter "a", focuses then on:

   1) calendaring and scheduling each employee to maximize her or his opportunities to develop professionally to serve students in a mastery-based, tech-supported, customized teaching, advising, and learning environment; and

   2) calendaring and scheduling all other school-community activities in service to the ideal of school-as-major-affinity group. This may be a low-conflict/no-conflict master calendar or schedule that supports work and life and school and home balance, e.g., childcare for employees, parents, and others in the community at any and every school-community event, which requires purposeful and constructive communication and support of all constituencies.

The 10 Correlative Success Predictors

1. **The year-round school—student.** Each student attends a minimum of 42 weeks. Older students "take classes" (meet with teachers and with one another) not just during traditional school hours, but in late afternoons or evenings, yielding a "business day" of 14 hours. The "business week" is six days. The term "homework" is obsolete. The school-in-business year is a minimum of 48 weeks. The years from matriculation to graduation vary, not only as a function of the calendar and schedule, but, critically, as a function of the schoolwide focus on mastery-based, tech-supported, customized teaching, advising, and learning. (See Part One, the three Meta-Predictors).

2. **The year-round school—faculty and faculty supervisors.** Full-time faculty members teach (engage students) 36–42 weeks, and participate in three to six weeks of professional development during which they do not formally meet with students. Teachers' year-round focus, during engaged-with-students periods and, equally, outside those periods, is on building advanced skills in leading students and one another in mastery-based, tech-supported, customized teaching, advising, and learning approaches.

Academic administrators focus on hiring, supporting, and evaluating teachers, while seeking to build a faculty culture of predictability and supportiveness consistent with the vector created.

3. **Highly specific teaching, advising, and professional-development-focused teacher contracts.** This is especially true in middle and upper schools, where teachers and learners are often onsite beyond traditional school hours, in service to customization not only of teaching, advising, and learning, but of teacher-student, student-student, and teacher-teacher scheduling. In some settings, the mix of full-time and part-time faculty approaches 50–50. This yields wide ranges in teacher remuneration and allows for higher salaries for full-time teachers without (necessarily) increasing the total compensation lines in the operating budget (due to the significant number of part-time, duties-specific, no-employee-benefits teachers).

4. **School Heads increasingly focused on leadership.** Management skill and experience are not enough. A central component in the successful headship is the leadership, coaching, and community-building function in which improving the capacity of others is a dominant theme. The Head's personal well-being and balance are also key.

5. **Boards thoroughly strategic in their operations.** Board structure and function is organized along the axis projected by the school's current strategic plan and strategic financial plan. These paired strategic documents are re-created from scratch every three-to-five years. They are constructed not only to address the standards implied in the ISM Stability Markers, but to address the implications for the Stability Markers of the three Meta-Success Predictors and the 10 Correlative Success Predictors.

6. **Boards, Leadership Teams, faculties, students and their families are increasingly at home** with, and proactive in regard to, teaching and practicing inclusion of those who comprise minorities (e.g., ethnicity, socioeconomic levels, learning differences, gender identification) in any school population. ISM's Student Experience Profile (expanded, as needed, to address individual circumstances) or similar instruments are in regular use to monitor students' experience of inclusion, and their experience of the overall predictability and supportiveness of their daily environment.

7. **Maximum available points on the key financial metrics identified in three of the ISM Stability Markers.** The overall mix of money used to operate (as distinct from money used for capital projects), including:

- cash reserves,
- debt,
- debt service,
- endowment,
- percent coverage of operations expense with hard income,
- annual fundraising, and
- funds earmarked to professional development

yields full credit on the appropriate Stability Markers' scoring metrics. The mere alignment of money with the Stability Marker metrics does not in itself have meaning, since the meaning is found in using the money metrics in ways consistent with the three Meta-Predictors.

8. **Technology budgets (less personnel costs) at 3%+ of the operations budget**. For schools that market themselves as technology leaders, the percent is higher. For others, 3% is the minimum annual allocation. This is necessary to address in full the Meta-Predictor No. 1 specification of year-round professional development focused on mastery-based, tech-supported, customized teaching, advising, and learning. (Note that only in cases in which these funds are used clearly in support of the Meta-Predictors do they have relevance to them.)

9. **Risk management analyses and systems in place and regularly updated.** The Meta-Predictors' implications for increased student-teacher engagement with outside organizations, more internships, more service learning, more outdoor programs, and more travel combine to elevate substantially the importance of risk management analyses, systems, programs, and internal and external risk-related education. Besides this, the school-as-community-center and as major affinity group underscores the necessity of the school being viewed as safe: safe in all ways and safe in all circumstances.

10. **Flexible, green, curriculum-driven facilities.** Facilities are readily adaptable to the transforming effects of technological advances; the interactive effects of curriculum, technology, and instruction; and the burgeoning need to honor the environment's fragility and its potential to become itself an effective teaching tool. This relates to the principle that the habitats where students and teachers interact have an important effect on learning potential.

The strategic and tactical implications of the three Meta-Predictors and the 10 Correlative Success Predictors for Boards of Trustees and School Heads are profound and far-reaching. Preparation, if not already underway, should formally begin no later than during your school's next strategic planning and strategic financial planning sessions. Moving forward in your school with your own expression of the three Meta-Predictors and the 10 Correlative Predictors is, in ISM's view, not optional. It is imperative.

The only question is the rapidity with which you choose to move forward. In the long run, maintaining strength on the ISM Stability Markers may not prove possible without having also made strides on the Meta-Predictors and the Correlative Predictors. Said differently, the Stability Markers may not prove sustainable at high levels without aggressive changes in your mission-delivery systems and all that goes with those systems.

Recruiting and Orienting Board Members

Profiling the Board

The viability and stability of a private school, regarding the Board of Trustees, relies on three factors:

- the understanding by the Board of its strategic role in protecting the school's viability;
- the relationship between the Board of Trustees and the School Head—and how that translates into each playing an effective and appropriate role; and
- the strategic recruitment of the Board with the mission of the school and the strategic role of the Board held to the forefront.

This chapter deals with the third of these points. Failing to recruit strategically—to profile the Board—may result in a motley group of people who cannot forward the school's vision or ensure its viability for the next generation of students. The typical definition of profiling—how the Board focuses on attracting expertise to strengthen its capacity to plan strategically and carry out its agenda—may lead Trustees to think in too limited a way. This process can certainly deter the Board from the haphazard process of suggesting names to fill vacancies based on a list of Board responsibilities (a financier, a legal expert, a major contractor, and so on). However, the Committee on Trustees, entrusted with this responsibility, must think in a much more intentional way about this process. (For more on this committee's duties, see the section on The Committee on Trustees in Chapter Nine.)

Imagine a much bigger picture. Board profiling is driven by the school's planning document, typically the strategic plan and strategic financial plan. These two Board documents talk about a four- to six-year horizon for thinking about the school's future direction. In them, the Board sets out clear objectives for sustaining and improving the school over that time, estimating potential costs and assigning responsibility for tasks. This last part—assigning responsibility for tasks—connects to Board profiling.

The question the Committee on Trustees must ask is: Whom do we need to fulfill the plan over the life of the plan? Consider means to foster relationships. Ensure a continuing succession of exceptional individuals who are at various stages of cultivation within the "Trustee Funnel" and being groomed to take on the challenges and responsibilities stated in the strategic plan.

Imagine the following example. One of the objectives outlined in the strategic plan of the fictional Exempli Gratia Academy is to run a capital campaign in Year Four. The objective is first to raise funds for a new Arts Center and second to build the Faculty and Staff Professional Development Endowment Fund. The Committee on Trustees recognizes the need to plan now (Year One) to ensure the support is there when the campaign kicks off (Year Four). It then identifies the need for:

- three major donors on the Board to give by Year Four,
- Major Gifts Committee development and support, and
- two (or more) passionate advocates for the school on the Board who have high community profiles.

See the following example of a general outline, Strategic Plan Mandates for Exempli Gratia Academy's Capital Campaign.

Strategic Plan Mandates for Exempli Gratia Academy's Capital Campaign				
Program	Year One	Year Two	Year Three	Year Four
Board members and significant donors	Prepare a list of potential supporters, working with the Development Director	Cultivate six prospects—invite at least three to work on a project or committee; donors will give to the annual fund	Continue cultivation; identify more prospects and begin the cultivation process	Invite three prospects onto the Board; others participate through the Development and/or Major Gifts Committee; continue cultivation
Major gifts	Prepare a list of potential supporters, working with the Development Director	Invite supporters to donate through the annual fund; develop strong ties to the school	Invite supporters to increase their donations through the annual fund	Invite supporters to increase their donations through the annual fund
Community profile	Develop a profile of the desired Board members	Cultivate community members through school involvement, committee work, and annual fund	Invite community members to join the Board; begin cultivation of the new group	Active membership by some; continue cultivation of others

The two tools that follow may be used or adapted by your school as you profile and build your Board to be a stronger and more effective organism that fulfills the mission of the school.

Tool One is the Committee on Trustees Planning Document. This time line tool uses the strategic plan to predict, assess, and validate the direction of the Committee on Trustees.

Tool One: Committee on Trustees Planning Document (with two examples)				
Item (from the strategic plan)	**Responsible Person/Entity**	**Presently Operating (yes/no) and Effective (1-9)**	**Cultivation Notes (reference to Tool Two)**	**Action Notes (reference to a time line)**
Create Board profile	Committee on Trustees	Yes 7	None in the pipeline	Profile one for 2019, one for 2020, one for 2021
Create Major Gifts Committee	Committee on Trustees and Development Director	No	John ready to join the Board and chair the committee; two in the pipeline	Invite John (by the Board President); invite two onto the committee (by John)—continue cultivation for Board membership; profile one for 2020 and one for 2021

Tool Two is the Committee on Trustees Confidential Individual Profile. Use this for the detailed and confidential assessment of potential Trustees. Assess the applicant on these 12 attributes, as well as on general notes that provide anecdotal reference to the person's increasing involvement in the life of the school.

Tool Two: Committee on Trustees Confidential Individual Profile (example)

Name of Prospect: Susan Junge **Present Relationship:** parent/donor/businesswoman

Item	General Competencies		Notes
Board membership with a view to becoming Finance Committee Chair when Anwar retires in two years	Work Ethic	excellent	Susan headed up the auction last year very effectively (bought items worth $1,250); she has volunteered on several occasions; she testified to the school's efficacy at an open house; donates to the annual fund (increased 100% over the past two years to a present $2,000). Susan is not a gossip in the parking lot; she values what the school stands for and has often expressed this privately and publicly; she deals with disagreements in an appropriate manner
	Wisdom	seems astute	
	Wealth and History of Giving to the School	six-figure household income; consistent donor at satisfactory level	
	Leadership	yes	
	Clout	well-connected in town	
	Mission Appropriateness	yes	
	Specific Competencies		
	Experience	15 years of running her own family business	Susan has demonstrated her financial skills through her volunteer activities as well as her astute questioning of the School Head last year concerning the Annual Financial Report. She has the capacity to ask hard questions without alienating people. We still need to find out more about her interest in the school long term rather than just as a school for her children.
	Profession	construction	
	Education	university BA	
	Strategic Skills	unknown	
	Interpersonal Skills	excellent ability to bring people together	
	Financial Skills	excellent	

Note: The three areas of general competencies, mission-appropriateness, and specific competencies must all be addressed. Deficiencies can be overcome in almost every area EXCEPT mission-appropriateness. If this factor is significantly lacking, this person should not be recruited.

The following two profiling principles, if carried out resolutely and with perseverance, ensure your Board is not just fully staffed, but replete with the wisdom, wealth, and work ethic to further your mission to the next generation of students.

- The profiling plan should cover the time line of your strategic plan (four to six years).
- Each individual to be cultivated should be assessed across a broad band of identified characteristics that, though they might look generic, are carefully considered with reference to the needs of the strategic plan.

Using the two tools, in tandem with these two principles, helps the Committee on Trustees focus clearly on the real difference-makers. This also helps ensure that each Trustee can be completely satisfied with the job he or she has been assigned to do.

A Due Diligence Checklist

As you profile the Board, you need to cultivate, elect, orient, evaluate, and at times counsel individual Trustees. Good governance defines a school's strategic direction and determines how to use its resources to achieve strategic goals. Within this context, Trustees must understand what is required to perform their duties: thorough due diligence. This term is familiar to Trustees who work, for example, in the worlds of investing or mergers and acquisitions. In our context, it refers to fulfillment of certain fundamental obligations in serving as a Trustee at a private school.

A Due Diligence Checklist identifies these obligations and assists in any of the following four ways:

- as a referent when cultivating and orienting new Trustees;
- when addressing Board function and, in particular, the adequacy of individuals' focus on strategic purpose during meetings of the full Board;
- as a checklist for evaluating individual Trustee performance (and, if needed, providing counsel); and
- as evidence of the Board leadership's own due diligence and prudent governance, which appeals to fundraising donors and prospects when they are cultivated.

Dr. David Hubbard, the former President of Fuller Theological Seminary in Pasadena, CA, identified four major roles of nonprofit Board members in an interview conducted by management authority Peter Drucker. (This interview was published in the chapter "The Effective Board" in Managing the Non-Profit Organization: Principles and Practices (HarperCollins: 1990).) These roles—Governor, Sponsor, Ambassador, and Consultant—have been applied in this chapter to categorize the responsibilities of private school Trustees. The items listed under each role create a set of due diligence competencies. Amend these items, as needed, to meet your Board's specific needs.

In the role of **Governor**, the Trustee exhibits:

- knowledge of (and ability to quote) the school mission statement;
- knowledge of and commitment to the Board's own mission statement;
- familiarity with Board bylaws;
- thorough preparation for meetings;
- on-time attendance at meetings;
- mental "presence" at—and full and active participation in—meetings;
- strategic focus in the content and process of meetings; and
- commitment to group process, the open exchange of ideas, and the presentation of a unified voice to constituents.

In the role of **Sponsor**, the Trustee exhibits:

- thoughtful inquiry into the financial soundness of the school's assets;
- promptness in making personal financial contributions to school initiatives (operating, annual, capital, and endowment) and providing support to all development and fundraising goals;
- understanding of the components of the strategic financial plan and their interplay; and
- scrupulous avoidance of conflict of interest.

In the role of **Ambassador**, the Trustee exhibits:

- enthusiastic public support for the school, its Head and administration, the faculty, fellow Trustees, and the Board as a whole;
- commitment to the confidentiality of Board matters;
- care and prudence in commenting on any Board matters in casual conversations; and
- openness to constituent contact, but with the understanding that he or she does not "represent" a particular constituent group.

In the role of **Consultant**, the Trustee exhibits:

- generous giving of time and talent when called on by the Board or administration. The school relies on the special training and skills the Trustee brings to the Board, especially those for which he or she was recruited;
- a willingness to keep up-to-date on best practices in private schools;
- contribution to the Board profiling processes; and
- commitment to Board-level diversity as the school defines that term.

Charge your Committee on Trustees with the review and revision of this Due Diligence Checklist for approval by the full Board. Provide each Trustee with a copy of your checklist and make plans for its formal use during your annual Board retreat. Include the document in your Board Policy Manual. The checklist, as amended to suit your Board, can become a living document to assist in maintaining your Board's strategic function and achievement of strategic goals.

The Caveats of Profiling Your Board for Wealth

Before we leave the topic of Board profiling, we must consider a final concern—profiling for wealth. Schools often dream about attracting Trustees with deep pockets. "If we could just get a few rich Trustees, our problems would be solved!"

But, as we've mentioned, the way you structure your Board membership must be designed to support your school's mission, as expressed through the strategic plan. Focusing on wealth—rather than mission—can prove to be problematic.

It's not easy to "profile for wealth." People of financial means have many demands on their time and generosity. They need to be "cultivated"—brought into the life and mission of your school in ways that link with their own interests and goals. You may also find that some well-to-do professionals (contractors, insurance agents, attorneys, public relations firms) would rather do business with the school than serve on its Board. They should not do both.

In profiling for wealth, the advantages to the Board, and to the school's bottom line and development efforts, are easy to see. (There's a reason it's one of the criteria.) However, mission-appropriateness and an excellent "fit" with the strategic plan's goals are just as essential. Schools overlook the potential disadvantages of overemphasizing wealth.

Wealth: The Plus Side

Trustees with wealth offer valuable assets, both as individuals and in their circle of relationships. They are excellent candidates for the Major Gifts Committee and can make substantial lead gifts for fundraising campaigns. Through their relationships, they have access to others with money and influence, and can encourage them to become major donors and serve on the Board.

Wealth: The Drawbacks

- Your school can become too dependent on a wealthy Trustee. When that person leaves the Board, hits a financial downturn, or decides to shift support to another cause, the school might face a budget crisis.

- There's another concern related to ongoing "bailouts." Successful people are interested in supporting success, not shoring up a struggling enterprise unable to attain firm financial footing. What happens when the Trustee is no longer interested in writing the check to bridge the gap?

- The school can end up under the Trustee's control, to a greater or lesser degree. What that Trustee chooses to fund is accomplished, whether it is in the school's best interests. For example, the Trustee might be able to guarantee donations to support construction of a new gym. But can the school pay for maintenance, utilities, insurance, and other associated costs over the years? And if the school's most pressing need is to upgrade technology, what impact does this have on the strategic plan?

- Others on the Board and in the school community may not be as generous because they know there's someone who will write that last check to reach the annual fund or capital campaign goal.

Board profiling is a powerful tool, one that allows your school to think deeply about the impact the Board can have during a specific strategic financial planning cycle. Carefully consider where wealth fits into your profiling efforts.

Board-Level Diversity

Your school's diversity efforts start at the Board level. Here, diversity can be addressed without the direct costs usually associated with achieving socioeconomic or socioethnic diversity in your student body, or diversity in your administration, faculty, and staff. The starting point is in your planning document, every iteration of which should call for developing a Board profile to fit the strategic or long-range plan. Open the way for a Board discussion of diversity, even for a broad topic like "Increase the socioeconomic and socioethnic diversity on the Board of Trustees." The process includes the following universal steps.

- Charge your Committee on Trustees with a periodic review of your planning document.
- Ask the Committee Chair to revise your previous Board profile to fit the new planning document, to facilitate the next stage of your existing document—in this case, including Board-level diversity as a goal. The resulting profile will typically call for "slots" to be filled with individuals to enhance the Board's diversity.
- Once the Committee on Trustees completes a new Board profile, place the drafted profile on the full-Board agenda for examination, discussion, modification, and adoption. (Do this in the same fashion as with any other significant new committee proposal.)
- Once the Board approves the new profile, charge the Committee on Trustees to:
  - spearhead the process of developing lists of individuals to match the profile;
  - cultivate those individuals to Board committee and to full-Board membership;
  - provide Trustee orientation for all new Board members; and
  - evaluate their Board and Board committee performance over time.

These steps and procedures comprise the Board profiling process and its follow-up activities under any circumstances. When Board-level diversity has become part of your strategic or long range plan, these generic steps will, of course, then include actions that are specific to that strategic or long-range goal.

Summarize in a four-item list what the Board President may choose to put into effect.

- Annually pull the "Board-level diversity" items from your planning document and place the items within the context of your annual Board agenda.
- From their position on the annual Board agenda, reformulate the items into a portion of the charge given to your Committee on Trustees. (For example, "As our committee develops its new Board profile, attend to the issues of socioeconomic and socioethnic diversity, consistent with our newly adopted strategic plan.")
- When the Committee on Trustees presents its newly drafted Board profile to the full Board for consideration, ensure the profile includes umbrella language: "In accordance with the implications of the strategic plan, the

profile slots indicated should be occupied by individuals who, as part of the overall mix, provide:

- a balance of affluence and nonaffluence (i.e., socioeconomic diversity);
- a geographical distribution encompassing our school's major "draw areas" for its student body;
- ethnic diversity reflecting our community's overall ethnic mix (i.e., socioethnic diversity);
- leadership potential that has been demonstrated in other contexts;
- influence within the overall community and within special segments of the community; and
- integrity, compassion, and a willingness to work toward the greater good."

(Here the profile proper—the recommended list of profiled slots—would begin.)

- As the Committee on Trustees launches the cultivation process, seek the most efficient combinations of "profile slots" and "umbrella considerations." For example, a real estate professional who also fits one or more of the umbrella considerations (e.g., affluence, ethnic minority, influence within the community) may be a more desirable target for Board cultivation than one who fits none of the umbrella considerations.

Success in achieving Board-level diversity does not guarantee subsequent success in achieving student-body diversity—or administration, faculty, and staff diversity. This approach is the most feasible starting point, however. The presence of diversity on the Board can alter the image of your school in ways that make the desired ripple effect more likely to occur.

Trustee Recruitment, Orientation, and Re-recruitment

An annual Board retreat provides the opportunity for Trustees to step back and devote a day specifically to planning. A well-planned and goal-centered experience can rejuvenate Board members, build teamwork and commitment, and refocus them on the tasks ahead.

A Board retreat offers many other benefits. As Trustees plan this event, they may want to include opportunities to:

- orient and integrate new members;
- create the annual Board agenda for the next 12 months;

- review committee structure and discuss how to develop it further;
- examine and prioritize the top two or three challenges the Board faces, and identify strategies for resolving them;
- think through the Board's relationships with the School Head, the Parent Association, and other constituencies;
- assess the school's long-term facilities and property needs, and begin planning for a major gifts program or a capital campaign; and
- above all, review the Board's basic purposes. This recommitment to its historic reason(s) for existing, coupled with any needed adjustments, is the foundation on which future decisions rest.

Planning Your Retreat

Whether you are setting up your first Board retreat or working to make your current process more effective, ask and answer the following nine questions to guide your thinking.

What is our rationale for proposing an annual retreat?

Which benefits and tasks are you unable or unlikely to accomplish at your regular meetings? Which could you address more successfully in the extended time frame offered by a retreat?

What time of year makes the most sense for an annual retreat?

The most common choices are early summer and early fall, at whatever point you can assure the best possible attendance. However, there is no "wrong" time of year to schedule a Board retreat.

Which weekend times prove to be most productive?

Your goals are to maximize both attendance and the Board members' energy levels. While the full-day Saturday retreat may be the most popular and workable, some Boards prefer a Friday evening and Saturday morning combination. The latter schedule leaves most of the weekend open, and the working time is roughly the same as in the full-day arrangement. A half-day is also a possibility. However, few Boards choose this option. If the goal is to have expanded time to think and plan, this approach doesn't offer much more meeting-and-discussion time than you would have in a regular Board session.

Which individuals or committee(s) will be asked to organize the retreat?

This responsibility falls to the Committee on Trustees. That's not to say that this group does all the planning and preparation. A lot depends on what you have on your agenda. Of course, the committee would handle the new-Trustee orientation and integration part of the retreat. In other areas, the committee would partner with the appropriate committees to prepare for sessions targeted to the various tasks and topics the Board will address.

For example, the Chair of the Committee on Trustees might ask the Finance Committee Chair to put together financial projections. If you're looking at faculty salaries, it would be worthwhile to have several scenarios that show particular levels of increase—and the resulting impact on tuition of each one. If you will be working on formal short range or long range planning, then an ad hoc planning committee may be in order. If setting the stage for a major gifts program or a capital campaign forms the agenda's core, then your Development Committee can take primary responsibility.

Where should the retreat be held?

The school may be the most convenient—and economical—location. It's usually not the best choice, however. Instead, consider a lodge outside your town; a conference room, perhaps at a Trustee's office or somewhere in the community (the local library, a restaurant, etc.); or a Trustee's home. Any of these can provide a more productive site. Moving away from the school, particularly if you hold regular Board meetings there, helps make the event "special" in participants' minds. You want them to arrive with higher and different expectations than those they bring to the routine meetings. A change in location is part of making that happen.

Will we need a facilitator for all or part of the retreat?

Sometimes bringing in someone from the outside helps create the "special" mindset so desirable for productive retreats. Apart from this, however, the basic question is whether facilitation will assist with achieving your goals and purposes for the retreat.

The term "facilitator" can be defined in two ways. One type is skilled in group process and provides assistance with moving the Board toward its goals within your time frame. Perhaps one goal for your retreat is to create a Board agenda for the year. The members would divide into groups, each assigned a specific task. The facilitator's role would be to circulate among the groups, keeping the discussions on track and providing perspective and guidance.

The other type of facilitator assists primarily with presentations (i.e., sharing information) on the relevant topics—such as the basics of Board structure and function or strategies for profiling new members. This third-party perspective can be a valuable tool, helping the Board think through areas where it has gotten stuck and putting it in a position to move forward.

The Friday-Saturday scenario works well with this second type of facilitation. The Friday night session can focus on presentation and discussion, while the Saturday morning follow-up is a true workshop. The Board spends that time working as a group to achieve one of its goals (e.g., creating an annual Board agenda or a case statement for a capital campaign).

What "homework" should we require of Trustees in preparation for the retreat?

This "homework" consists of material encouraging thoughtful consideration of the Board's and school's future course. Depending on your goals, it might include the results of a parent-satisfaction survey, a survey of the Trustees themselves, a demographic analysis, an accreditation report, an independent assessment, or a financial analysis.

What follow-up should we plan for the retreat?

Be sure to give just as much consideration to this element as you do to your plans for the retreat itself. You will invest well over 100 person-hours in your retreat. Plan for a vigorous follow-up so Trustees retain the sense of "time well spent" and forward momentum produced during the retreat.

At the next regularly scheduled Board meeting following the retreat, begin with a well-prepared review of the retreat process and of the decisions you reached or the plans you developed. Assign those decisions or plans either to existing committees for brisk action or to one or more ad hoc committees formed specifically for those purposes.

How much should we budget for the retreat?

Establish a budget with a high-side estimate designed to cover any retreat you anticipate holding in the future. That way, your annual budgets can always include a figure generous enough to support a successful Board retreat. If less is spent, those dollars will simply drop to your bottom line's surplus at year's end.

A well-planned and well-executed annual Board retreat serves as one of the key ingredients in enhancing the focus and the quality of your Board's overall function and effectiveness. The eventual beneficiaries of your enhanced Board-level focus will be the students who experience the strengthened programs and facilities that result.

The Board Committees

Board Committee Structure and Function

Your Board's committee structure, far from set in stone, should be flexible and emanate from the school's quadrennial strategic plan. Some committees—such as the Finance Committee—will always have tasks to accomplish. The strategic concept, however, is that there are few standing committees in the old sense of being listed in bylaws as necessarily in operation indefinitely, with a permanent set of responsibilities listed in the bylaws committee-by-committee. The extreme codification of Board structure is a poor fit for ISM's "strategic Board" concept, in which most Board committees' tasks are delineated annually and, as a rule, have their antecedents in the school's strategic plan.

Three primary facts undergird this approach.

- It is the most economical method for accomplishing the Board-level components of the strategic plan (while the School Head and the administration attack the operations-level components of the plan).

- Each Board committee member is assigned an actual responsibility, the successful discharge of which has real consequences for the school's forward movement.
- The Board and its committees are transformed almost immediately into a task-focused organization, as distinct from a bureaucracy whose committees exist primarily because the bylaws say they must, and whose committee tasks have no necessary relationship to the strategic plan.

Determining the Structure

In late spring or early summer the Board President should meet with the Committee on Trustees (with the School Head present) to develop the Board committee structure for the coming school year. Board bylaws may specify some aspects of that structure. However, if you have moved toward ISM's "strategic Board" concepts, your bylaws will allow considerable latitude in setting up the Board committee structure in ways most likely to advance your strategic plan.

Begin with your annual Board agenda-setting process. At this session, next year's Board-relevant strategic plan items are identified and listed on the Board agenda for implementation. Every Board committee (existing and potential) is subject to scrutiny as you ask and answer the question, "What essential function will this committee fulfill in the coming school year?" Your answers to this critical question will produce a Board committee structure conceptually similar to the Sample Board Organization Chart shown below.

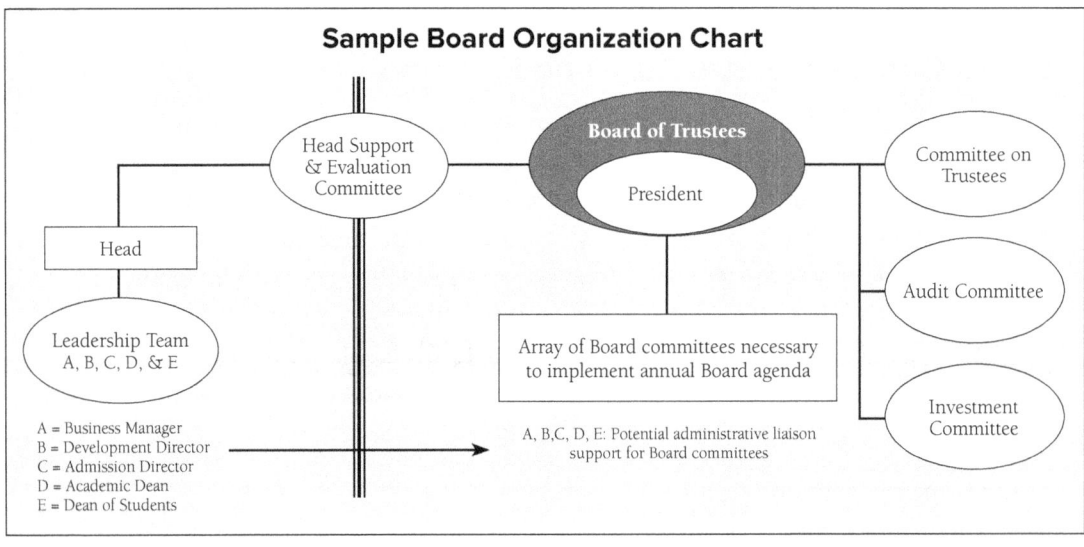

Two Critical Committees

The Committee on Trustees and the Head Support and Evaluation Committee deserve special comment. The Committee on Trustees:

- "profiles" the Board's "mix of membership" (list of necessary characteristics) at least as often as producing a new strategic plan. This is in contrast to the traditional Nominating Committee's annual question, "Whom can we get to fill that empty seat?";
- cultivates appropriate individuals to produce a Board membership that conforms to that profile;
- spearheads the annual Board self-assessment;
- plans and organizes the annual new-Trustee orientation;
- plays the lead role in developing the annual Board retreat; and
- serves as the Board President's primary source for advice and counsel regarding overall Board structure and performance, as well as individual Trustee performance.

As the accompanying chart implies, the Board executes its operations-oversight function through the Head Support and Evaluation Committee. This committee makes the annual judgment as to whether the School Head has made everything "right and good" to the greatest (reasonable) extent possible. The Head Support and Evaluation Committee privately evaluates, and the full Board publicly supports, the School Head. The committee forms the interface between the Board's efforts to govern and the administration's efforts to manage. The chart demonstrates this, positioning the committee on the dividing line between operations and governance.

In an annual summer session (or series of sessions), the Head proposes to this committee his or her major management-focused goals for the upcoming school year—many of them grounded in the strategic plan. The Head and the committee negotiate a short, but high-impact, list of goals. (The annual Head Support and Evaluation Committee's goal-setting process should be collaborative. But, in the rare case of an actual impasse, the School Head "loses." The committee reserves the right to insist that a given goal be included in the evaluation process for that, or any, year—even over the Head's opposition.)

For each of these goals, the committee should ask, "How can we determine that this objective is being met?" Answering that question helps the committee develop its own data-collection process for the year. This design becomes the Head Support and Evaluation Committee's modus operandi and determines the quality of the evaluation. If done well, the evaluation will be immensely helpful to the Head, providing information that he or she has no other way of obtaining. At the same time, this process allows the Board to discharge its primary governance and management responsibility. (Keep in mind that Form 990 compliance has specific requirements of the Board concerning the School Head. The Board must complete an annual CEO compensation comparison to ensure the compensation is "reasonable and not excessive." This process must also be documented in the Board minutes. Consult with your legal counsel to make sure your school has the proper 990 processes and reporting procedures in place.)

As the chart further indicates, the members of the Leadership Team (senior administrators reporting to the School Head) will staff each Board committee. The Business Manager, for example, will serve as administrative liaison for the Finance Committee.

Two "special" Board committees deserve notice here, because they are "standing committees" in the traditional sense. One is the Audit Committee; the other is the Investment Committee. These are unusual Board-level committees in ISM's strategic-Board concept in that neither is engaged in furthering the strategic plan in any direct sense. They are necessary for responsible Board operation. Both stand in a somewhat independent relationship to the Board as a whole, and typically report to the Board infrequently (perhaps twice a year).

Many Boards operate with an active Executive Committee. A high-performing Committee on Trustees and a high-performing Head Support and Evaluation Committee leave an Executive Committee with nothing to do. Beyond that, active Executive Committees—those that meet often—tend to disenfranchise the rest of the Board members. (This statement does not apply to the standard "emergency" Executive Committee function wherein the President, Secretary, and Treasurer, forming a de facto committee, are authorized to take action for the Board under unusual circumstances. This emergency function is an important one, and should always be bylaw authorized.) We will discuss the Executive Committee in more detail later in this chapter.

The foundation for ISM's recommended strategic Board structure and function is a qualifying strategic plan. The plan, to qualify, must incorporate the operations-finance correlates of the strategic plan at every point. The net tuition gradient, the operations expense gradient, the operations bottom line, and other critical variables are all readily abstracted from the document and expressed concisely on a single Excel sheet. With the strategic plan and its accompanying strategic financial plan in place, your Board can operate as a goal-focused governing body, the heart of which lies in its task-focused, annually revisited and revised committee structure.

The Committee on Trustees

ISM is often asked its perspectives on succession planning at the Board level. ISM's views on this are grounded in a long-established set of conclusions about the relationships between Boards and institutional excellence. These views—more accurately, ISM conclusions—strongly emphasize "Board-as-task-group" over "Board-as-bureaucracy." Thus, while ISM opposes the oft-used corporate concept of succession planning per se, we support succession *training*.

ISM's position has little to do with the most common approach to this, i.e., future Board Presidents serving first as Board Vice Presidents. There is an inherent problem with the whole concept of "vice president," and the problem is apparent in many organizations, not just Boards of Trustees: Other than presiding in the absence of the President, the position's responsibilities are elusive.

Thus, ISM has never been sanguine about the existence of the Board Vice President position, and recommends instead creating a vigorous, prestigious, and strategically critical task unit called the Committee on Trustees. If you have this committee in place—by any name, of course (Governance Committee and Committee on Directors are among the common alternatives)—then you already have the ideal succession training platform for future Board Presidents. If you have never created a Committee on Trustees, then you are missing one of the most fundamental ingredients of a strategic Board (i.e., a Board with a structure and function that correlates strongly with long-term, mission-specific excellence in private schools).

In this succession training context, consider the following steps.

1. **Use the Committee on Trustees in part as an apprenticeship committee.** If your current committee has, say, three members, consider asking the Chair to invite one or two leadership-promising Trustees to sit in on selected meetings. The Chair might refine this approach by inviting one Trustee who is new to the Board and one who has several years of experience. The Chair presumably would want them present especially at meetings at which the committee is:
   – scoring the annual or twice-annual administration of ISM's Strategic Board Assessment instrument, which will inevitably be coupled with a discussion of the outcomes and their implications;

- reviewing the current Board profile and beginning the work of crafting a fresh one (see the next section in this chapter); and

- beginning to plan the next new-Trustee orientation.

2. **In a Committee on Trustees meeting at which no apprentices are present, the Chair should have the members discuss which Trustees—whether serving in the apprenticeship capacity or not—show the most promise as future Board Presidents.** Suggest that they schedule private interviews early on—long before it is time for the Board President to rotate out of the position—with any individuals so identified. Discuss with your Chair the fact that the committee must make clear that this is an exploratory interview only; the whole Board will ultimately elect its new President. Suggest that, in the interview sessions, the committee cover the principles of the strategic Board, using the Strategic Board Assessment, if helpful, and discussing the detailed implications of this instrument.

3. **When it comes time each spring-summer to form and reform Board committees, consider moving one or more of the apprenticed Trustees and early interviewed Trustees onto full membership on the Committee on Trustees.** This allows your prospective Board Presidents to immerse themselves fully in the fine points of your Board's structure and function. This includes observing and discussing the performance of individual Trustees (a subject not normally broached in the presence of a committee apprentice).

In ISM's research study on Board leadership, the core findings illustrated the dramatic differences between successful leadership of the private school governance unit, on the one hand, and the School Head position, on the other. Effective leaders among School Heads demonstrated a host of personal characteristics viewed by their employees as critical (e.g., they were seen as morally upright, self-effacing people, able to give public positive reinforcement effectively). Effective leaders among Board Presidents were simply those who were willing to organize the Trustees into a strategic unit, and to operate consistently within those strategic parameters.

This does not suggest, of course, that personal characteristics do not matter. It suggests, rather, that the School Head is "on" all the time, highly visible to those in the school community. The Board President is usually behind the scenes, visible primarily to her or his Board-level colleagues, and even then mainly in Board meetings. Personal characteristics, thus, take a back seat to an individual's strategic and organizational interests and abilities.

Succession training under these circumstances is best viewed as comprising part-time—and eventually full-time—service on the Committee on Trustees. This is the unit charged with assisting the Board President in analyzing, organizing, and troubleshooting Board structure and function.

The Committee on Trustees Calendar

There is a predictable cycle of tasks the committee can expect to undertake in most years. (Boards occasionally face tasks of such magnitude that a standard Board calendar cannot realistically be followed, such as a year in which the search for a new School Head is conducted.) Following is a suggested calendar that has proven workable in most years for most Committees on Trustees. This calendar assumes that:

- there is a strategic plan and strategic financial plan in place;
- ISM's Strategic Board Assessment is in use as a set of guidelines for strategic Board structure and function;
- a Board profile has been created in response to implications of the strategic plan; and
- an annual Board agenda and an annual operations agenda are in place and in use.

If these essential components are missing, you may find it difficult for your Board to operate in a strategic fashion (i.e., explicitly supporting the school's long-term viability and sustainability) and, thus, difficult for your Committees on Trustees to set up a calendar that helps ensure continued, strategically focused Board structure and function.

October through February

- **Cultivation of Board-profile-implied new members:** Most Boards elect their new members in the spring, induct new members near the end of the school year, and hold their new-Trustee orientation sessions in summer or early fall. The winter months tend to be those during which prospective new members are identified (based on the Board profile) and cultivated to membership. The cultivation process includes a prospect interview during which potential new members are sounded out on their willingness and ability to commit to the core expectations of trusteeship.

- **Midyear Board assessment:** A midyear Board evaluation consists simply of the Committees on Trustees using the annual Board agenda as a report card to summarize progress-to-date on each item listed. Some committees actually use A's, B's, and C's and so on in the report; others compose a verbal summary of progress on each item. Either way, the objective is to assist the Board in discussing its progress, and to develop midyear corrections when needed. A midyear self-evaluation, on the other hand, consists of the committee administering ISM's Strategic Board Assessment as a monitoring device for the "strategic-ness" of Board operations. Some committees administer the instrument, while others simply talk the members through the instrument, using it as a discussion guide.

- **Review and update of key Board documents:** As a natural follow-up to the midyear Board evaluation and self-evaluation, consider holding a Committee on Trustees meeting in which the central agenda item is your Board's key documents: their location and the need, if any, for updating them. Incorporation papers, bylaws, current and past strategic plans and strategic financial plans, bond covenants, investment policies, and the Board policy manual represent but a handful of the array of documents, past and present, whose locations should be known. Board policy manuals, in particular, are often allowed to become outdated simply because the committee's annual calendar does not call for their review.

March through May

- **Preparation for the summer retreat and new-Trustee orientation session:** As Committee on Trustees Chair, schedule these paired events early enough to ensure that all Trustees have the meetings on their calendars, and so that detailed planning can proceed. A frequently used approach is to hold the new-Trustee orientation on a Friday late-afternoon or evening, followed by the full-Board retreat on Saturday morning, or all day Saturday. In this way the new Trustees can hit the ground running when the retreat begins. Often the retreat focuses on the annual Board agenda: the agenda-driven committee charges, committee assignments, committee calendars, report dates, and proposal dates. You will also, of course, want to consider the social elements of the annual retreat, including the setting and its ancillary components, e.g., a faculty-appreciation luncheon. (Jewish day schools rework this schedule to observe the Sabbath.)

- **Nomination and election of new Trustees:** This is the formal culmination of much that has preceded: Board profile, identification of individuals, cultivation, potential new-Trustee interview. If you have kept your Board members informed throughout, actual nomination and election are routine steps leading toward your summer new-Trustee session.

- **Participation in counseling out of ineffective Trustees:** If your committee has identified one or more ineffective Trustees, the committee Chair has the responsibility of discussing—first with the rest of your committee, then with your Board President—the process of counseling out any individual Trustee who is not (or no longer) serving appropriately or effectively. ("Counseling out" is preferable to "voting out," a step that is taken when the Trustee in question refuses to resign and when the destructive institutional, social, and political consequences of retaining the Trustee outweigh the fallout from forcible removal of the Trustee.)

- **End-of-year Board evaluation, self-evaluation, and officer election:** Procedurally, this replicates the midyear evaluation and self-evaluation discussed previously under the October-through-February heading, using the expiring annual Board agenda and the Strategic Board Assessment as points of reference. This year-end process is often coupled with a look into the coming school year by presentation of a draft annual Board agenda and, consistent with this forward look, presentation of the new-officer slate for discussion and vote.

June through September

Recommendations for the upcoming year's calendar and work: The Committees on Trustees members should prepare recommendations for the President's consideration on the following:

- finalized annual Board agenda;
- Board-meeting calendar;
- Board-committee leadership; and
- Board-committee membership and charges.

Leadership of the summer retreat and new-Trustee orientation: The highest-visibility event of this time period will be the long-planned annual Board retreat and the new-Trustee orientation. As noted under the March-through-May listing above, a Friday evening new-Trustee orientation coupled with a Saturday retreat allows your new Trustees to be integrated swiftly and efficiently into the Board's work.

As noted in the opening paragraphs of this article, the calendar just presented is a suggested one that has proven workable in most years for most Committees on Trustees. But its assumptions are crucial, that there is:

- a strategic plan in place;
- a set of Board-operations guidelines that uses ISM's Strategic Board Assessment as its framework;
- a Board profile built on the strategic plan's implications; and

- an annual Board agenda and annual operations agenda that plot the strategic work of the year.

With these basics in place, your Committees on Trustees calendar can support and sustain strategically focused Board operations year after year, to the long-term benefit of the school you serve.

The Head Support and Evaluation Committee

There is a strange paradox in the process of supporting and evaluating the School Head. Yes, the School Head is the Board's only employee. That means the Board must hold her or him accountable. But the Board is unable to do that! Think of everything the Head is responsible for overseeing:

- the entire academic program,
- the entire athletic program,
- the cocurricular program,
- human resources,
- facilities,
- re-recruitment and recruitment of students,
- marketing of the school,
- parent relations,
- development,
- evaluation,
- legal matters,
- health and safety issues,
- scheduling,
- janitorial services, and
- food services ... and the list goes on.

The point here is that it's just not possible for the Board with its competencies to oversee the School Head effectively. Furthermore, the job is so enormous that if you tried to evaluate on the exceptional fulfillment of all these tasks, chances are most Heads would fail! So the questions "Who evaluates?" and "What do they evaluate?" are important ones. The Board must answer them!

The best practice is to delegate this task to a special committee of the Board called the Head Support and Evaluation Committee. It serves an advice and counsel function. The criteria for membership of this committee is specific.

- You have significant CEO-like leadership experience (e.g., in a small business, a large United Way campaign, a symphony Board, or a division of a medium-sized corporation).
- You are a strategic thinker, demonstrating that in your contributions to committee and Board work.
- You have a reputation for supportive, positively reinforcing behaviors.
- You have absolutely no special or private agendas of your own.
- You are neither hostile to, nor a sycophant of, the School Head.

Selection of the committee members is all-important. The Head Support and Evaluation Committee is chaired by a Trustee. However, the rest of the slots can be filled by those best qualified to fill the role, Board or non-Board. For example, the current or former Head of a noncompeting private school might serve as a non-Board member of the committee. Note that the "support" function is so critical that the Head can be given an informal veto power over the selection of members on the committee. (However, if abused, this courtesy will be withdrawn.)

The following sequence of steps outlines the process.

The Board reviews the strategic plan annually and writes the annual agenda.

The School Head writes the annual administration agenda, drawing from:
- the Board annual agenda (strategic plan and strategic financial plan);
- unfinished planning document items from the previous year(s); and
- any other major operational initiatives.

As with all Board committees, formally charge the Head Support and Evaluation Committee annually and in writing. The committee members, with the School Head, agree on the five or so objectives drawn from the annual administration agenda (and, hopefully rarely, aspects of the Head's performance that must be addressed) on which to evaluate the Head. These objectives are not due diligence items—matters that the Head is expected to fulfill as part of normal job requirements. They are objectives that will make a difference in the life of the school.

The Head Support and Evaluation Committee then reflects with the Head on his or her commitment to the school mission, particularly as it relates to the Head's own personal and professional objectives. Ask the Head to consider strengths and weaknesses that should inform the coming year's objectives and derive a professional development objective from those. Add that to the five objectives. The committee establishes data points that will denote progress, completion, and success for each of those objectives (including the professional development objective). Finally, it creates a time line that shows when the Head and the committee will meet to talk about progress, seek support, and move to success.

This document is then presented to the Board for information (not approval, given the Board has already approved the strategic plan and strategic financial plan from which the Head's objectives ultimately are derived). Some Boards and Heads choose, in addition, to publish these objectives in the school newsletter. This is a good idea. It makes sense to educate your constituents about the Board's and Head's direction for the year in terms of gaining support for them and in managing expectations around directions that are not being taken.

The Head Support and Evaluation Committee then continues to monitor the process regularly throughout the year. It is good practice to meet monthly. The committee reports to the Board as to how well the Head has met the objectives—typically this will be a happy report! There will be no surprises though. The support in the committee represented by that monthly meeting means the data collected through the year will predict success as the year progresses. If there is a surprise at the end of the year, someone made an error!

Is there a different way to do Head evaluation? The typical method is to:

- carry out some form of 360-degree survey where people's opinions of the Head are solicited (Note: 360-degree surveys are never to be used for evaluative purposes for the Head or anyone else in the organization—only for professional development purposes);
- hand out a form at a Board meeting at some point in the spring for Trustees to complete; and
- have a discussion based on the information gleaned from the surveys and the filled-in forms.

The weaknesses of this alternative approach are many. Evaluation conducted this way tends to:

- be related to the school's strategic plan only incidentally, if at all, and thus is not constructed around the Head's basic "job description"—fulfilling the school's planning document;
- use criteria that are unwritten, unspoken, and, typically, known only after

the fact (by the Head and perhaps by most of the Trustees);

- rely for the most critical judgments on the Trustees themselves, regardless of whether the Trustees have been engaged with the Head or with the school in ways likely to produce informed judgments;

- rest, in whole or in part, on using a checklist or a rating form repeatedly, from year to year, despite the evolutionary nature of the school's, and consequently the Head's, performance requirements;

- move toward judgment only: that is, it seldom displays characteristics that could be termed "developmental" (which, being developmental, would foster improvement in Head and school performance during the school year); and

- be mostly subjective and impressionistic—measurable objectives and data relevant to those objectives are seldom incorporated into the process.

Remember that support and evaluation of the Head is one of the Board's most important roles. It must be done effectively, respectfully, and supportively. Doing it well furthers the institution's goals and cements a proactive relationship.

The Finance and Audit Committees

ISM Consultants often hear the phrase "the Board has fiduciary responsibility." This phrase merely means that each Board member has the legal responsibility to act solely in the best interests of the school they serve. To facilitate good fiscal stewardship, we recommend two finance-oriented committees to assist the Board in this crucial area: the Finance Committee and the Audit Committee. Let's explore their roles.

The Audit Committee's functions are distinct and focus on creating and overseeing financial policies. It's roles include:

- the review of financial statements and other official financial information provided to the public;
- the assurance that all reports are received, monitored, and distributed correctly;
- oversight of the school's internal controls, including management's compliance;
- risk management—assessing risk and determining appropriate mitigation;
- oversight of the annual independent audit process, including engaging the

auditor and receiving all reports;
- review and submission of the annual IRS Form 990 and all forms and schedules; and
- assurance there is a whistle-blower policy and a process by which it is communicated and monitored.

The Audit Committee has important responsibilities assisting the Board with oversight of financial controls and policies. However, it is not within the committee's purview to plan or conduct routine examinations of the school's financial operations. The management is responsible for those operational tasks.

The Finance Committee is strategically and tactically oriented. The committee's roles include oversight of:
- preparation for all budgets and financial statements;
- the administration, collection, and disbursement of financial resources;
- the Board concerning the making all financial decisions;
- preparation of the Form 990; and
- implementation of conflict of interest, document retention, whistle-blower, and executive compensation policies.

Many independent schools combine the roles of the Audit Committee and the Finance Committee into a single committee, frequently with the name Finance Committee. However, since the implementation of the Sarbanes-Oxley Act, enacted in 2002 as a reaction to several major corporate and accounting scandals, separating the duties of these committees is recommended. This brings a natural check and balance into the fiduciary role—the strategic role of making policy and the management role of action and implementation—and helps assure the entire Board of sound fiscal process.

Last, it is important that the Board impanel Board members with financial expertise. Each of these committees must comprise at least one such expert. This can include those with financial degrees or professional experience that qualify them. With large budgets and sizable endowments, it is mission-critical that the Board lead for success. Impaneling people with fiscal knowledge and expertise is not only prudent, it's mandatory.

The Development Committee

A Board member who serves on a dynamic Development Committee is in for a truly meaningful experience. When this group is successful, it directly enhances the education of each child.

Know what this committee is supposed to do! As a member of the "development quartet" (the School Head, Board President, Development Director, and Development Committee Chair), it's your job to get this group on track with training, strong leadership, and a plan.

By providing the Development Committee with a clear direction and focus, you'll ensure that it avoids the three most common blunders.

- The Development Director is our committee's employee.
- Let's have another spaghetti dinner at $20 a plate.
- Parents can't afford tuition; why ask them for a donation?

What You Need in a Development Committee

The ideal Development Committee is a powerhouse—a group of dedicated, well-connected individuals who understand their roles in the development and fundraising process, and who carry out those duties with the school's best interests in mind. While this is a Board committee, it may also include members of the wider community who have the expertise and willingness to forward the school's development efforts.

Based on the following outline of these areas of responsibility, how effective is your school's Development Committee?

1. Strategic Board

The Development Committee's initiatives grow out of the goals set by the Board of Trustees in the strategic plan.

- Create the development plan (as it relates to the school's strategic and financial plans), and keep it updated on an annual basis.
- Set goals within that context for annual, capital, endowment, and planned giving.
- Reflect on and assess the committee's effectiveness in fulfilling its various responsibilities.
- Contract for outside services (e.g., feasibility studies, development audit).
- Develop Trustee education programs related to development and include them in the annual retreat each year.

- Participate in the orientation program for new Trustees.
- Identify potential Trustee candidates for the Committee on Trustees.

2. Leadership

- Take personal responsibility as a development leader.
- Respect the Development Director's leadership role.
- Cooperate with the Development Director as the School Head's representative on the committee.
- Assist the Development Committee Chair and Development Director in identifying the key volunteer leadership for school fundraising efforts.

3. Case for Support

The case statement explains to donors, clearly and concisely, why money is needed and how it will be used, invites people to invest in the school, and describes how their gifts make a difference.

- Monitor the school's ability to raise money through periodic data gathering from constituent groups.
- Develop and test the school's Case for Support.
- As the professional staff develops internal and external marketing strategies, support them by brainstorming and offering feedback.
- Provide consistent feedback to all constituent groups on the outcomes of development efforts.

4. Prospects

- Profile prospects based on the needs of the development plan.
- Identify individual prospects who fit the profile, and enable them to be part of the school's development efforts.
- Bring individuals closer to the school, wherever they are in the Donor Cycle.

5. Plan of Action

- Recommend policy to the Board (e.g., a gift acceptance policy).
- Apply that policy (e.g., in approving solicitation programs).
- Recommend the development plan to the Board for approval.
- Develop an agenda and an annual calendar based on the plan.
- Be effective in carrying out that agenda.

6. Donor-Centered Programs,

Annual Fund
- Support the Development Office in the annual fund campaign, either directly or through a subcommittee.
- Provide leadership for the Annual Fund Cabinet, the structure of development professionals and volunteers who carry out this event.
- Assist in profiling actual and potential donors.
- Make personal gifts in support of every major fundraising effort.
- Educate the Board about the primary importance of the annual fund.

Major Gifts
- Set up a subcommittee for major gifts.
- Make personal calls to cultivate actual and potential donors capable of giving major gifts.

Using the Outline

Besides guiding the Development Committee, this outline can be used to create a clear job description for specific components of the school's development program. If you are seeking members for the Annual Fund Committee, a job description might read:

- participate in drawing up the development plan;
- attend all Development Committee and Annual Fund Committee meetings;
- make a personal gift before the official annual fund kickoff;
- serve on the Annual Fund Cabinet; and
- be positive, optimistic, and a believer in the school's mission.

For a Major Gifts Committee member, the job description might look quite different.

- attend all Major Gifts Committee meetings;
- make a leadership gift to the annual fund;
- cultivate two or three other major gift donors; and
- make a major gift to the capital campaign or support special needs of the school as they arise.

The list of responsibilities also proves helpful as you look ahead, profiling and cultivating potential Development Committee members. Consider how you can provide them with increasingly greater opportunities for leadership within the school's development orbit and, finally, bring them onto the committee.

When the Development Committee is clear about its role, creates an effective plan, and views development as a long-term process, it stays on track. The members avoid the common blunders because they operate on the basis that:

- the Development Committee and the Development Director have complementary and supporting roles;
- development is about cultivating relationships and connecting donors' values with the school's mission; and
- parents get excited about supporting fundraising activities when they are clear that the goal is to enhance their children's education.

When the Development Committee operates on these principles, giving increases, your school's leadership depth is enhanced, and the members' service on this committee is a truly satisfying experience that bonds them even more closely to the school.

The Buildings and Grounds Committee

Rather like the Finance Committee, it is hard to imagine a school that would not have a Buildings and Grounds Committee. Its role is complementary to the Finance Committee, caring for the current facility (including grounds) and planning for the facility's development, reinvention, and sometimes expansion into the future.

Do not limit membership of the committee to Trustees. The composition depends on the needs of the strategic plan and strategic financial plan, as laid out in the Board's annual agenda and the Buildings and Grounds Committee charge. Consider the following guidelines.

1. The Chair should be a Trustee.
2. The Vice Chair should be a Trustee in training for the Chair's position.
3. One member should also be a member of the Finance Committee to coordinate the strategic financial plan and annual budgeting process.
4. The Business Manager and Facilities Manager are voting members.
5. There should be at least two non-Trustees.
6. The size of the committee (at least six members) should reflect the work it must do.

Create a rubric for annual evaluation of the Buildings and Grounds Committee's work (see the accompanying chart), and to ensure that no element is forgotten.

Use the score to:

- inform the Stability Marker metrics;
- provide guidance around priorities;
- compare progress from year to year; and
- give more energy than a yes or no might provide.

	Buildings and Grounds Evaluation Rubric		
Element	**Definition**	**Max Score**	**Actual Score**
Facilities Audit	There is a facilities audit and it is updated annually.	10	
	We communicate PPRRSM needs on a five-year rolling basis to the Finance Committee.	10	
	Each year's facility needs are met.	20	
Master Campus Development Plan	There is a Master Campus Development Plan and it is up to date.	5	
	The Master Campus Development Plan is in use.	5	
Land Acquisition Plan	There is a Land Acquisition Plan and it is up to date.	5	
	The Land Acquisition Plan is in use.	5	
Safety	The Buildings and Grounds Committee has a school safety walk checklist.	10	
	The Buildings and Grounds Committee does a safety walk around the school once a month.	10	
	Action items are remedied in a timely way.	20	
Insurance	Appropriate property insurance is in place and monitored annually.	10	
Risk Management	There is a Business Continuation Plan and the committee monitors it annually.	10	
	Insurance is in place to pay for facilities to keep the school operating in the event of damage.	5	
	Grand Total	**125**	

Attend to all items and any deficits built into the quadrennial strategic planning process and into the annual administrative agenda. Note that this committee includes both strategic and operational components. The committee must understand that it functions as a Board committee and must look to the Board for its charge to operate and makes recommendations to the Board for action (specifically in reference to the Stability Markers). It also functions as a school support committee and thus makes recommendations to the School Head for action. It has no power to act unilaterally outside these constraints.

The Buildings and Grounds Committee must understand that safety is foremost in the minds of parents. While it is not the committee members' responsibility to consider emotional and social safety, physical safety from a facilities point of view is a crucial aspect of the committee's task. Consider the following observations from tours ISM Consultants have undertaken.

- Doors to the roof not locked.
- No ability to access eyewash stations in science laboratories due to obstructions.
- No crash bar on doors leading to the outside.
- Chemicals in cabinets that were not locked in rooms with no supervision.

The Buildings and Grounds Committee's ability to "see" these kinds of things and remedy them is crucial to the risk management process. While other elements of its charge are strategic and can be done over months or even years, the safety walk-around is a monthly activity that needs vigilance and constant attention.

The Buildings and Grounds Committee also has a vital role to play in implementing the purchase of property or developing new or renovated facilities. In these circumstances, it may wish to expand the membership of the committee for the duration of that work and ensure it has appropriate expertise to advise the Board.

The Buildings and Grounds Committee's job has several facets:
- planning that impacts the strategic plan and strategic financial plan (Campus Master Development Plan and Land Acquisition Plan);
- annual planning impacting next year's budgeting (facilities audit); and
- safety and risk management (business continuation, insurance, and safety processes).

Working as a volunteer-professional partnership ensures that the school has mission-appropriate facilities that meet the needs of this and the next generation of students, a key element in supporting the Board's viability objective.

The Executive Committee: Vestige of Bureaucratic Governance

A "strategic Board" focuses on the long-term viability of your private school, i.e., on financial planning, organizational planning, facilities planning, capital and other campaigns, and the array of components integral to those planning themes (including institutional performance on the ISM Stability Markers). For many years, ISM has emphasized the importance of the strategic Board, and, thus, the central roles of the Committee on Trustees and the Head Support and Evaluation Committee. We have intentionally excluded the Executive Committee in our description of the strategic Board's structure.

ISM's reasons for this follow.

1. With a high-functioning Committee on Trustees and Head Support and Evaluation Committee, there is little remaining for a day school's Executive Committee to do. (Boarding schools, with Trustees scattered around the nation and the world and thereby unable to meet face-to-face more than two or three times per year, must for that reason have active Executive Committees.)

2. An active Executive Committee, such as one that routinely meets between full-Board meetings, tends to disenfranchise the rest of the Board. It often appears to other Trustees that critical decisions—including the content and ordering of the full-Board agenda—are made by the Executive Committee. In such circumstances, attendance at full Board meetings often suffer.

3. Executive Committees tend to comprise the Board President, one or more Vice Presidents, a Secretary, and a Treasurer, a bureaucratic arrangement usually spelled out in bylaws and marginally, if at all, related to the governance-level structure and function implied in the quadrennial strategic plan and strategic financial plan. That structure and function, reviewed and adjusted each year in the annual Board agenda and in written Board-committee charges, reshapes the Board annually to conform to the action called for in the strategic plan. (At the operations level, the corresponding document is the annual administrative agenda.) Often the Vice President is the designated successor to the office of President. Yet, it is in service on the Committee on Trustees, not on an Executive Committee, that a Trustee learns the intricacies of the workings of the strategic Board—as distinct from the bureaucratic Board. It is on the Committee on Trustees that an individual is best prepared to succeed in the presidency. (The President, Secretary, and Treasurer should be listed in the bylaws as a unit authorized to take action in circumstances in which full-Board canvassing is impractical. Often this is simply to authorize the School Head to write a check for more than his or her policy-dictated limit. This limited-

function Executive Committee is not what ISM means by an "active" Executive Committee, and should exist in some form on all Boards.)

4. The Executive Committee is usually populated by some of the most talented Trustees on the Board. This is a poor (i.e., not talent-specific) use of such individuals. These high-capacity individuals should serve on:
    – the Committee on Trustees;
    – the Head Support and Evaluation Committee;
    – the Finance Committee;
    – the Development Committee;
    – the Facilities Committee; and
    – other critical Board units (those which normally carry the burden of moving a given strategic plan and strategic financial plan forward on a month-by-month basis).

Give careful thought to your Board's structure and function. Consider the extent to which it is an action-oriented organization. Then move forward, as appropriate, to convert your organization into one built around:
    – a multiyear strategic plan and strategic financial plan;
    – a high-functioning Committee on Trustees;
    – a high-functioning Head Support and Evaluation Committee; and
    – a small handful of annually generated Board committees, usually starting with finance, development, and facilities.

The long-term beneficiaries will be the faculty, the families, and the communities served by your school.

The Education Committee: Justifiable?

A perennial question discussed by school leaders is the "validation" of a school's student programs: curriculum, cocurriculum, pedagogy, vertical alignment, and other components in a private school's mission-delivery system. After all, any school's mission has its strongest impact in classrooms and on playing fields.

The near-universal method for establishing meaningful student-program validation is the recurring accreditation-agency review. This peer review asks and answers the basic question: "If this is your mission, what evidence can we, the accreditation team, find that your curriculum, cocurriculum, pedagogy, professional development and evaluation, and other systems support that mission, and at what level of excellence?" ISM's perspective is that the Board's most helpful role at this point is to:

- review the accreditation report and its recommendations;
- ascertain which of the recommended changes or enhancements have "price tags"; and
- layer those changes into the next strategic plan and strategic financial plan, if this can be done without jeopardizing the school's strategic financial integrity.

Changes or enhancements of this sort, having been enabled financially by the Board's planning decisions, will be implemented by the Leadership Team and faculty. In this case—as in most cases—the linking unit between governance and operations, according to standard ISM-recommended practice, is the Head Support and Evaluation Committee of the Board. This unit would thereby serve as the Board-to-administration oversight agency in the ongoing validation and implementation process.

The Board President may have already pondered whether—in addition to the accreditation review and enhancement process—the "validation" question warrants creating an Education (or Academic or Curriculum or Student Program) Committee. Perhaps some of your Board colleagues have suggested that there is a need for an ongoing Board-level review-and-recommendation process, entirely separate from the periodic accreditation-team visits.

ISM urges caution. In ISM's experience, this Board-level committee tends more often to hinder rather than help any "mission-validation" effort, in part by its very existence.

Faculties understand the chief executive is the School Head. They stand ready to work with the Head and his or her second- and third-level administrators on projects having to do with mission validation and enhancement of student programs. To introduce a governance-level committee into that equation is inherently confounding in faculty members' eyes.

What, for example, will a Board-level Education Committee do with its validation-related recommendations, once it has developed them? Will it deliver its proposals to the School Head with the expectation that the Head will then instruct his or her second-level administrators and the faculty as a whole to implement these proposals? The organizational disconnect between (strategic) governance and (operations) management virtually guarantees skepticism and resistance from the faculty, and, in the worst cases, the actual subversion of any such proposals.

Beyond this, the existence and actions of such a committee can create a burden for second-level administrators. They can feel called on to report to Trustee Education Committee members on programmatic matters, duplicating what they "report" to the School Head, and often, in the process, opening the door to Trustee "suggestions," suggestions which, in effect, circumvent the School Head entirely. The potential for organizational confusion and for subsequent organizational dysfunction is high.

An Alternative

Trustees and administrators often feel a need to validate the adequacy and excellence of student programs in ways other than those addressed by regular accreditation review and the normal (operations-level) follow-up actions. If so, consider including a pertinent item in the next (quadrennial) strategic plan and strategic financial plan. (If your bylaws call for the existence of an Education Committee, consider a review of your bylaws to make them more consistent with the structure and functions of a "strategic" Board of Trustees.) Let's say in Year Three of the new plan items call for creating an ad hoc group to conduct a "mission-validation study" in preparation either for the regularly scheduled Year Four-Year Five strategic planning event upcoming, and for the next accreditation-team visit (depending on the scheduled time frames of these two events).

Ensure that your strategic plan calls for the School Head to serve as the chairperson of this ad hoc group. The group will, of course, include faculty members, other administrators, and, plausibly, one or more Trustees. An ad hoc unit that is chaired by the School Head is not, by definition, a Board committee. It is an administrative task unit with (if the Head chooses and if you agree) one or more Trustees helping to populate the unit.

This approach, unlike creating an Education Committee, does not distort organizational lines of authority and responsibility, nor does it prove confounding to the faculty. The ad hoc unit will, no doubt, keep the faculty and the Board apprised of progress. When the report or proposal is finished, the unit will share the outcomes with those groups. Finally, as appropriate, all or portions of the document will be shared with the school community in general. Operations-level implementation can then proceed along regular school-organizational lines without attendant drama or confusion.

When Board Committees Fail

Committees are the linchpins of an effective Board. When Board meetings are well-attended, purposeful, and gratifying, this foundation usually grows out of understanding and applying the principles of properly establishing committees.

The key to success is identifying, recruiting, and managing strong leaders—a critical role shared by the Board President, the Committee on Trustees, and the School Head. Committees are only as strong as the people who lead them.

But what happens when committees fail? Often, even if a committee's original charge for the year is comprised of feasible goals, it may get sidetracked and fail. Why? The fault is probably the committee Chair's—and, in these cases, "fault" usually means less an outright dereliction than simply an instance of mediocre leadership.

Successful midyear intervention, by the Board President or the Committee on Trustees, may be required when a committee has problems. This may take the form of renewed training for the committee Chair, renewed orientation for the entire committee, or a complete redirection and new staffing of the committee. The latter may include appointing a Co-Chair. However, to be successful, this appointment usually requires an endorsement from the original Chair.

There are instances in which the Board President takes over the problematic committee and leads it to a successful and timely completion of its goals. Or the overall Board agenda is simply not met that year. For most Presidents in most years, the "worst solution" approach is better than the "no solution" approach.

But take care! Often what is perceived as failure by a committee is actually a failure of the Board. Effective committee work can be torpedoed by a Board that listens to a committee's proposal and then proceeds to redo or alter that work. The committee members then become frustrated—as do other Trustees, who feel the committee did not do its work well enough.

Reduce the likelihood of such unhappy results by following these guidelines for creating written and oral proposals.

- Explain how each committee interpreted its original charge.
- Describe the plan used to address the various items of the charge.
- Mention the roles played by individual committee members and subcommittees.
- Show the sequence of steps that led to a narrowing of focus and emerging conclusions. Note the degree of challenge involved by quoting the number of person-hours, communications, and meetings. Also detail the significant contacts made and the resources studied.
- Show the major conclusions, listed in descending order of importance.
- End with a draft resolution designed to focus the following Board discussion and vote.

When Board members receive little more than a one-page list of conclusions and a resolution, a sense of superficiality can result. The approach suggested here, orchestrated by the committee Chair, highlights the process, building a foundation for the findings that resulted.

Clearly, properly selecting committee Chairs is well worth the time and effort to foster strong leadership. That leadership forms the bedrock for the Board's success and progress.

Sample Board and Committee Calendar

The following sample calendar is descriptive, not prescriptive, and is not intended to be exhaustive.

Month	Board	Committee on Trustees	Finance	Head Support and Evaluation	Development
April	Meeting; Board self-evaluation	Counsel out ineffective Trustees; prepare for summer retreat; effect the self-evaluation process by the Board	Review tuition fee schedule as necessary from the strategic financial plan		Review progress of annual fund campaign: set goal for next year; review strategic financial plan and identify objectives
May	Meeting	Nomination of new Trustees	Review monthly reports from the Business Office	Develop annual objectives for the Head	Select Chairs for coming campaigns; plan materials for Development Office to produce over summer
June	Annual retreat; approve agenda for the year	Annual Board evaluation; recommendations for any changes in structure; lead retreat	Review monthly reports from the Business Office	Provide report regarding Head's carrying out of previous year's objectives	Confirm Development Committee members for the coming year
July-August		Trustee orientation	Study and approve the school's annual audit		Review and identify leadership gifts
September	Meetings begin with strategic focus		Review Business Office procedures; prepare summary reports for the school	Monitor and support Head in carrying out objectives	Board and faculty solicitation complete; annual campaign kickoff
October	Meeting	Cultivation of profiled Board prospects	Review monthly reports from the Business Office	Meeting	Phonathon and personal solicitation
November	Meeting	Ensure effectiveness of whole-Board meetings	First-draft budget presented	Meeting	Phonathon and personal solicitation
December	Meeting; budget approval	Follow-up orientation	Budget presented to Board		Conclude annual campaign
January	Semi-annual retreat		Review monthly reports from the Business Office	Semi-annual retreat	Review reports
February			Review monthly reports from the Business Office	Meeting	
March	Meeting	Update Board profile based on strategic plan	Review monthly reports from the Business Office	Meeting	Repeat the process

CHAPTER TEN

Board Meetings and Other Functions

ISM has long stressed the fundamental importance of Board-level strategic planning, coupled with annual Board (and administration) agenda-setting, as being critical for a school to sustain long-term programmatic excellence. Stable schools have strategic Boards. Link these tenets explicitly to such organizational practices as Board profiling, new-Trustee orientation, bylaw revision, formation of a strong Committee on Trustees, and Board self-evaluation.

This chapter extends further the set of core ideas implied by ISM's own strategic Board concepts and practices to explore a set of guidelines for the conduct of "strategically focused" full-Board meetings. The Board President should consider adapting these guidelines for your own school's situation. Understand that these are not bylaw-level lists, but are suggested for inclusion in a Board policy and procedures manual.

Guidelines and Reminders for All Trustees

Consider a set of guidelines similar to these to steer your Trustees toward a strategic mindset when approaching any full-Board meeting.

- Anything that requires a Board vote goes to the top of the agenda.
- Set the agenda well in advance (reference the annual Board meeting calendar). Communicate additions to the agenda in the form of a request to the Secretary or Board President one week before the meeting. This point applies not just to annual Board agenda-related items, but to "old and new business" items as well. Limit the meeting to topics on the agenda.
- Trustees should refrain from using the captive audience of the full-Board meeting to bring up issues that can (and should) be worked out in committee. The full Board assembles for the primary purpose of receiving and acting on committee proposals and other, less formal, committee recommendations.
- The preceding guidelines notwithstanding, suppose a Trustee decides to raise an issue that does not appear on the meeting agenda. Perhaps the issue will require full-Board discussion and decision (as distinct from, for example, offering public congratulations to the Head for a noteworthy success). The Trustee should come prepared with a time estimate for the impromptu discussion, a proposed solution (or suggested pathway toward a solution), and an explanation regarding the need to introduce the issue immediately. The Board President, in consultation with the Chair of the Committee on Trustees, determines whether this last-minute addition can be admitted.
- When a Trustee is on the agenda to present a proposal to the Board, she or he must come well-prepared.

The following template assists in organizing a proposal presentation.

A Template for Full-Board Presentations

Share these components with your fellow Trustees, and remind them of the need to prepare for the session well in advance. Send formal committee proposals electronically or by mail to all Trustees a week before the meeting, so the ideas can be reviewed.

- **Purpose of the presentation.** Briefly describe what strategic plan goal or annual Board agenda item your presentation supports (e.g., presenting the results of the alumni parent survey: supports development of comprehensive Parent Education Plan).

- **Background.** In one or two paragraphs, outline the research (include supporting documents) conducted to reach the recommendation or proposal (e.g., X number of alumni parents were selected for the survey; Y number of alumni parents responded).

- **Board action requested.** What do you wish the Board to do with the information, recommendation, or proposal you are bringing before the members? If you are uncertain, consult with the Board President well in advance.

- **Financial implications.** Does your recommendation or proposal have a financial impact (e.g., on tuition or on the annual fund goal for next year)? Is that financial impact included already within the parameters set by the strategic plan and strategic financial plan? Have you consulted with the Chair of the Finance Committee on this question? If the two of you conclude that your recommendation or proposal calls for an adjustment in the strategic financial plan, ask the Finance Committee Chair to address that issue as part of your presentation to the Board.

- **Recommendation for action.** What exactly is your suggested action? What are the ramifications of moving forward in the manner you suggest? What alternatives have you explored? Why is this the best choice?

- **Impact on other Board-level committees or on the administration.** Does implementing your recommendation or proposal impact other units of the Board or the school management? Have you consulted with the affected leaders (i.e., committee Chairs and School Head), so their responses are known?

- **Comments.** Include any other pertinent remarks or supporting documents that seem useful. Incorporate a concise statement of the consequences of failure to act, unless that has become apparent when discussing the alternatives earlier in the presentation.

Action-Oriented Agendas for Successful Board Meetings

At many private schools, a typical Board session is often characterized by:

- lengthy discussions, often focusing on minutiae or items of special interest to just one or two members;
- a detailed report by the School Head on school activities since the last Board meeting;
- an inability to deal effectively with important issues because members do not have the background information they need;
- poor attendance—at times not even a quorum; and
- minimal progress—Trustees can't seem to take action or make decisions.

To plan for a more efficient, productive Board meeting, start with the agenda. Keep the framework focused on action, and set the stage for a successful session.

A Typical Board Agenda

Boards often undertake each meeting's work based on the same standard agenda, which encourages results that are not action-focused. Does your Board's agenda resemble the "Typical Agenda" in the accompanying figure?

This approach conveys a minimum of information. There is no indication that anything nonroutine in nature will be addressed. No suggestion that any topic should be researched in advance. No estimate of the time commitment to be made, nor of the time allocated to any particular topic. There is no focal point. Even committee Chairs with little to report will be expected to say something to fill their spot on the agenda. Members are not led away from any pet issue they may have, so they consequently can be expected to introduce it at the first opportunity.

Typical Agenda
Agenda Item
1. Call to order
2. Approval of previous minutes
3. School Head's report
4. Committee reports:
a. Committee on Trustees
b. Head Support and Evaluation Committee
c. Facilities Committee
d. Development Committee
e. Finance Committee
5. Old business
6. New business
7. Adjournment

An Enhanced Board Agenda

Board meetings can be exciting events in which Trustees are fully engaged, focused on significant issues, and oriented toward action. This is possible when Board operations are based on the concept that the majority of the Board's work will be accomplished at the committee level, rather than by the full Board. A strong committee system guided by carefully selected committee Chairs does the groundwork—discussion, fact-finding, recommendations. Then, in its meetings, the full Board can focus on action.

The "Enhanced Agenda" in the accompanying figure encourages that action. It specifies the key topics to be considered at each meeting, rates all agenda items in terms of importance on a scale of 1 (low priority) to 4 (high priority), and sets a time frame. The rating, carried out by the Board President and the Committee on Trustees Chair, with the School Head's input, trains the Board to focus its energy on items that are truly important.

Enhanced Agenda		
Agenda Item	**Time**	**Urgency**
Call to order	7:00	1
Approval of previous minutes	7:01	3
Review of Head's summary report	7:05	3
Discussion of one in-process committee issue	7:15	4
Discussion and ACTION on one committee proposal	7:20	4
BREAK	8:00	
Miscellaneous items for brief discussion and referral to appropriate committees	8:15	3
Action minutes summary	8:55	4
Adjournment	9:00	1
*Urgency—1 = low priority, 4 = high priority		

Note that this agenda specifies discussing only one in-process committee issue, taking action on only one proposal, and limiting the meeting to two hours. Although you may at times have more than two pressing matters to consider, sticking as closely as possible to these parameters helps ensure a productive, upbeat session.

Email the agenda to all Trustees at least four days before the scheduled meeting, as part of a packet that also includes a summary report of administrative activity prepared by the School Head and a digest of committee research or other relevant background for anticipated deliberation.

A Step-by-Step Look at the Enhanced Agenda

School Head's summary report. Since this report on administrative activity will have been sent to Trustees in advance, with the agenda, 10 minutes should be adequate time for a brief review and a pertinent question or two. The Chair of the Head Support and Evaluation Committee joins the Head in responding to any questions.

In-process committee issue. The purpose of this discussion is to allow a committee Chair access to whole-Board feedback about some sticking point faced by that committee as it works toward finalization of its proposal. For example, as the Finance Committee develops its proposed operations budget for the following school year, it may wish to have input from the whole Board on some particular expenditure under consideration. In another scenario, if the Development Committee is charged with putting together a strategic marketing plan by, say, December 31, it may want an in-process review by the whole Board in mid-November. This Board review of committee work is quite different in its purpose from the deadly habit of having every committee routinely summarize its activities, regardless of the nature and stage of development of those activities.

Discussion and action on committee proposal. This item is shown on the agenda in boldface and awarded a high rating on importance to emphasize to Trustees that this constitutes the primary reason for having this meeting. Members, duly alerted, can then be expected to invest significant homework time in preparation. (This material is the "digest of committee research or other relevant background for anticipated deliberation" that is sent in advance with the agenda packet.)

Miscellaneous items for brief discussion and referral to appropriate committees. Nonagenda issues raised during this segment of the meeting (the "new business" portion) should almost always be referred immediately to appropriate committee members or school administrators, or placed on the agenda for the next full-Board meeting. Again, the emphasis is on work in committee. Unless the item has true urgency and must be discussed now by the entire Board, it should not be pursued in this meeting.

Summary of action minutes. At the close of the meeting, the appropriate Board officer reads the action minutes, the short list of items on which action has been taken. This would include consensus approval (or not) of the in-process committee activity discussed in this meeting, the results of the whole-Board vote on the committee action proposal, and the referral to committee members or school administrators, or to a subsequent whole-Board meeting of any nonagenda items introduced in the "miscellaneous" discussion segment of the agenda.

Thinking About Your Board Culture

The Board President should thoughtfully consider the impact of these guidelines on the culture of your Board. Every organization, even one as small as a volunteer governing body, has a culture that implicitly condones or opposes certain ways of going about its business. It thus implicitly condones or opposes significant changes in those ways of doing business.

If these strategically focused guidelines for the conduct of Board meetings would do violence to your Board culture, you may want to begin with a session with your Committee on Trustees. This group, charged with shaping Board composition, structure, and function in support of the organization's strategic direction, is exactly the right starting place. It can assist you in defining the cultural (and other) impact of such guidelines on your Trustee organization.

This session may lead you to soften your Board's proposed guidelines, to include the Committee on Trustees in what could become a co-presentation to the full Board on the importance of such guidelines, or to sequence implementing the guidelines so that the Board can more gradually become accustomed to operating in this fashion.

A Board that adopts a strategic approach to its work in theory, but does not substantially alter its approach to its own meetings to conform to that theory, risks changing itself in words only. A set of concrete guidelines, enforced by the President and by the Committee on Trustees, implies that you are serious about moving your Board and your institution forward.

Board and Committee Attendance

Whatever type of school—country day school, academy, parent cooperative, Montessori, religiously affiliated—governance is based on volunteer commitment.

While it's impractical to expect Board members to arrange their personal and business lives completely around the Board's meeting schedule, they still must take this responsibility seriously. How can you emphasize the importance of attendance at both regular sessions and committee meetings without treating Trustees like truant students? Let the facts speak for themselves.

Have the Chair of your Committee on Trustees maintain a chart that shows the attendance record for all members, yourself included. (See the accompanying sample chart for the fictional Exempli Gratia Academy.)

This approach is not a panacea—it will not solve attendance problems. However, distributed quarterly to the members and formally reviewed during the Board's annual retreat, the chart does provide you with an excellent tool. For the members, it makes an appeal to their conscience and ego. For you, it serves as a warning system and an indication of when action should be taken.

Board members tend to be busy, involved, and important people. They have many legitimate demands on their time and can easily rationalize skipping a meeting. But it's also important that they be reliable and do a good job. Seeing the attendance record set down in black and white encourages them to make a self-appraisal.

Those whose attendance is borderline or worse may:
- not realize how many sessions they have missed—the chart will serve as a wake-up call;
- find that they are overcommitted and need to decide about where best to put their time and energy;
- have experienced a lifestyle change—a new job or promotion may require additional business travel, or personal or family responsibilities may impact their ability to serve;
- have decided that, since overall attendance has been slipping, showing up for meetings is not a priority;
- not find their work with the Board fulfilling; or
- have simply lost interest in serving on the Board.

Put the Chart to Work

The chart gives you and the Board members a tool to evaluate participation. Review it periodically to spot any problems that might be developing. Keep an eye on your own attendance record—it must be exemplary.

The Committee on Trustees Chair should bring the chart to the annual Board retreat for review. Those with perfect or near-perfect attendance records will be proud to have their commitment recognized and will be encouraged to maintain it. For those who need to improve, it's an opportunity to discuss the situation and solutions.

Faced with the facts, some members may decide to resign—with or without your encouragement. However, others will recognize the problem and resolve to take their commitment to the school more seriously in the future.

Board Attendance Chart
Exempli Gratia Academy—May 2018–April 2019

Name (committee assignments)	Term Expires	Board Meetings								Committee Meetings							
		1	2	3	4	5	6	7	8	1	2	3	4	5	6	7	8
Fred Crowley, Pres. – Finance – Buildings & Grounds	This year	X	X	X	X	E	X	X	X	X O	X O	X X	O X	X	O	X	X
Roberta Jones – Major Gifts – Public Relations	This year	X	X	X	O	X	X	X	X	X X	X O	X X	X X	X	X		
Marcia Delvecchio – Development – Committee on Trustees	Resigned	X	X	O	←	—	Resigned			X O	X X	O E	←	—	Resigned		
Mike Matsumoto – Development – Committee on Trustees	Next year	Joined→			X	X	X	X	X	Joined→			X X	X X	X		
Jerome Price – Marketing – Buildings & Grounds	Year after next	X	X	E	X	X	E	E	E	X O	E X	X E	X				
Eliza Proaño – Public Relations – Major Gifts	Year after next	X	O	X	X	E	X	O	X	E X	X X	X X	X O	X	O		

X = attended **O** = absent **E** = excused*

*out-of-town travel, on business, or personal or family emergency

Meeting Dates	Board: 5/17, 6/21, 8/16, 9/19, 11/15, 1/17, 2/21, 4/11 Buildings & Grounds: 6/5, 7/6, 9/4, 3/8 Committee on Trustees: 5/29, 8/8, 10/4, 1/10, 3/19 Development: 6/6, 9/18, 10/17, 11/7, 2/13, 4/5	Finance: 6/16, 8/24, 10/3, 10/24, 11/3, 11/24, 2/12, 3/30 Major Gifts: 6/15, 8/24, 10/9, 12/4, 3/28, 4/9 Marketing: 9/19, 10/16, 11/30 Public Relations: 5/29, 8/10, 11/29, 3/28

Identify the Causes

If your attendance-related discussions at the Board retreat focus on the last three items in the list, failure to attend meetings is merely a symptom—you face more serious problems. To make their work with the Board a priority, the members must:

- feel they have a personal stake in the success of the Board and the school;
- understand the essential part their participation and dedication play in keeping the school viable;
- respect one another and experience a sense of teamwork;
- find the atmosphere at meetings is friendly and supportive; and
- be confident that all meetings will be significant—well-run, issue-oriented, and "strategic," i.e., focused on the future rather than day-to-day minutiae.

When Board members understand their role and responsibilities—and when meetings are collaborative, action-focused experiences—these volunteers are more likely to make attendance a priority.

Maintaining an attendance chart provides a clear look at the situation, for you and your Board members.

Refocus Your Board Agenda and Minutes

There is a close relationship between the quality of your Board-meeting agenda and your Board-meeting minutes. If one of those is done in a perfunctory or unfocused manner, so, often, is the other. Frequently the Board-meeting agenda is, in fact, merely a generic outline that is retained for meeting after meeting with little attention given to it from one session to the next. That being the case, the meetings themselves may become formless discussions of whatever topics come to mind, a meandering process that will sometimes be reflected in formless, meandering Board-meeting minutes.

The Committee on Trustees should consider a refocused approach to both. You have a Board-leadership obligation to:

– use these talented Trustee-volunteers' time and energy as efficiently and meaningfully as possible;

– serve your school with a focus on those elements of institutional excellence that teachers and administrators cannot manage effectively for themselves, e.g., excellence in strategic planning, strategic financial planning, master facilities planning, comprehensive campaign planning, and the full array of strategic areas far removed from—but indispensable to—day-to-day, mission-centric teaching and learning;

– help your Trustees concentrate on committee-heavy research, proposal development, and ultimately whole-Board action; and

– provide Board minutes that accurately reflect this strategic and action-oriented approach to Board purpose, structure, and function.

Necessary to all this is the foundation on which Board activity and Board record-keeping should be built: a strategic planning document with a strategic financial spreadsheet providing the plan's quantitative implications. Once these foundation documents are in hand, a fully focused approach to Board meetings and Board minutes becomes much easier to accomplish.

Your annual Board agenda, constructed (usually) in late spring or summer in anticipation of the upcoming school year, lays out in simple, bullet-point format the strategic plan components to be implemented that year by the Board itself (rather than by the School Head and Leadership Team). Once listed and sequenced in the annual Board agenda, the actionable components of the Board's work that year fall readily into place and, as a result, so do the actionable components of the year's individual Board meetings.

With a crisp, action-focused approach to meetings, your Board minutes can reflect these same qualities. The minutes should:

- list those in attendance, those absent, and guests present;
- note when any person joins the meeting or leaves the meeting (so that there will always be a record of those present for a discussion or for a vote);
- incorporate committee reports or proposals as attachments that are referenced in the body of the minutes;
- record the disposition of any committee report (e.g., to be revisited at the March Board meeting);
- record motions with explicit reference to who made the motion, who seconded the motion, and what the vote total was; and
- show a successful motion—one that carries—in boldface, then include the successful motion separately at the end of the minutes with the heading, *"Action item: The strategic marketing proposal was passed by 18-2 vote."*

When the draft of the Board minutes is completed, it should be reviewed by the Board Secretary, the Committee on Trustees Chair, and the Board President before being circulated electronically one week before the next Board meeting. When the minutes are approved or approved-as-amended in the subsequent meeting, the Board President's and Board Secretary's signatures and date make the minutes official.

Board-meeting agendas and Board-meeting minutes reflect each other's tendency to be either strategic-action focused or formless discussions followed by formless records of those discussions. Refocus both these critical components in the life of your Board. Your colleagues on the Board will be grateful, and your school will be the long-term beneficiary.

Board Confidentiality

If your Board has not experienced the frustration of leaks of information about sensitive matters, your situation is rare. Probably, you are already familiar with the sinking feeling of discovering that a delicate Board discussion has become general knowledge among either students or parents, perhaps within 24 hours.

Board members are privy to sensitive information, most of it pertaining to strategic matter. Boards, by their nature, regularly discuss critical and controversial issues: e.g., tuition gradients, tuition-assistance levels, the school's (often changing) demographic mix, salary gradients, employee benefits, staffing levels, curriculum additions or deletions, personnel-position additions or deletions. When information about these issues—and others—circulate often before your Board has decided on any of them, rumors can race through the community before you even know that leaks have occurred.

ISM has long advocated a concept of trusteeship that suggests that Boards have "no living constituents." The only group a Board of Trustees can be said legitimately to represent is unborn children, children who will have a chance someday to experience your school's mission. This means that your Board does not represent the current parents, the alumni, the students, the employees, or any other element of the school community, present or past. (This is not the same as saying the Board should not be responsive to these groups when appropriate. It is to say the Board does not "represent" these groups as it would if it were a congressional body, elected by constituents, as with U.S. public schools.)

Private school Boards of Trustees hold the "trust" of the mission in their hands, figuratively, for future generations of students and families. Confidentiality of Trustee meetings is a core component in operating in ways consistent with the trusteeship concept and definition. Members must be able to discuss, debate, and decide about strategically weighty matters without fear that their words will be disseminated in the community, generating controversy and pressure from those who think of the Board as a public-school (constituent-representative) entity.

The Board President must regard the Committee on Trustees as a partner in keeping the confidentiality issue front and center. Many Committees on Trustees use item No. 15 in ISM's Strategic Board Assessment instrument (see Chapter Thirteen) as a guide for formulating an annual pledge sheet. All Trustees sign at the start of each school year. In the process of distributing the pledge sheet and discussing it carefully, a strong Committee on Trustees uses role-play and example to make certain that each Trustee is prepared—that is, practiced—in the art of dealing appropriately with constituents' (intentional or unintentional) efforts to elicit confidential information from them. At this session, mention electronic communication and the importance of prudent and careful handling of formal and informal documents about Board business (e.g., meeting minutes, emails).

A portion of that annual (or more frequent) discussion focuses on each Trustee's family. While the question of how to deal with Board-related information and process within each family has no standard answer, ISM knows that many serious issues of confidentiality involve leaks initiated by the spouse of a Trustee. Heightening each Trustee's awareness of this fact, and discussing various approaches, helps your Board members think through their at-home situations.

Keep in mind that, when leaks do occur, it is often impossible to determine the source. When a particular Trustee is at fault, she or he may not even realize it, or recall having made the slip. However, if repeated indiscretions can be traced to a specific member, then the Board President must counsel that individual and, if necessary, counsel him or her off the Board.

Maintaining appropriate communication with parents, faculty, and the community in general can help ease the pressure on Trustees to share what has occurred during meetings. Constituents must (a) understand the Board of Trustees deals with strategic decisions that determine the institution's stability and positioning in the marketplace; and (b) receive regular communication about Board decisions. They are less likely then to harass individual Trustees for their "secrets."

The Board Chair, assisted by the Committee on Trustees, should emphasize consistently the need to speak with one voice. The annual Board agenda, developed each late-spring or summer from your strategic plan and strategic financial plan, lays out the year's work of the Board systematically. This agenda can form a ready point of reference for your "one voice," e.g., "consistent with the annual Board agenda's fall schedule, the combined Board, administration, and faculty ad hoc committee has completed its work on the revised strategic marketing plan. Document highlights will be published on the school website after final review and proofing is completed, probably by midmonth."

Before each Board meeting ends, consider holding a brief discussion to determine what aspects of the meeting you will communicate to the community. You might collectively decide that continued work on a bylaws revision deserves mention in your website summary paragraphs, but that details still under discussion will not be included. Readers will recognize that they are receiving a partial report, but they will appreciate being given general knowledge of the Board's activities. They will, as well, be implicitly instructed regarding what a Board of Trustees does and does not deal with.

Confidentiality does not come naturally or easily to many individuals who are (otherwise) ideally suited to the role of Trustee. Help these gifted individuals understand the risks in allowing Board-level information into the community prematurely, and then give them the concepts and the language necessary to protect the integrity of your Board's discussions and decisions.

Board Meetings & Other Functions

Board-School Head Relationships

A reasonable contractual agreement between the Board and its sole employee, the School Head, encourages moderation, compromise, and perspective. While some feel contracts promote distrust, the opposite is true. The document, properly designed and implemented, will enhance the relationship between the Head and the Board by bringing clarity, focus, and mutual benefit to the most critical employment relationship of the school.

Boards can develop excellent relationships with their School Heads based on three core principles. The Board must:

- treat the Head in a predictable and supportive fashion;
- work reciprocally—that is, carry out its own duties with the same assiduousness as is expected of the Head; and
- ensure that it operates strategically to enable and support the Head to act operationally.

The School Head contract must define relationships, solidify the Board's expectations of the Head, and spell out specific spans of time. Any agreement should go both ways. The interests of each party must be served—with the "clients" (parents and students) as the ultimate beneficiaries.

The School Head contract should address at least the following main points. (Of course, other negotiable contract stipulations can be incorporated as your school sees fit or necessary.)

- Make specifics of salary and benefits absolutely clear.
- If either party fails to satisfy the stated conditions, the contract should provide for consequences. There should be no doubt about the school's financial obligations to the Head over the remainder of the contract.
- Clearly outline the performance evaluation process.
- Establish explicit time frames for renewing (or not) the contract, with parameters for resigning or seeking other employment.

The Two-Year, Rolling Contract

Set up two-year, rolling contracts—agree on each contract the year before the current contract expires. Just before the end of the first year of employment, set the stage for a renegotiated contract. The new contract supersedes the remainder of the first contract and continues through the following academic year. This sequence ensures the agreement never shrinks to less than a 12-month span (unless termination is real or likely), and may cover up to 24 months.

The Negotiation Process

Negotiations rarely happen after signing the first contract. New contracts are just extended from the previous one. At the same time, many Heads and Trustees are uncomfortable with contract negotiations. They are wary of entering what they may deem an inherently volatile process. Carry out the negotiation in a proactive way that establishes the school's care and concern for the well-being of the Head and his or her family.

The Support Process

The two-year rolling contract and continual examination of the Head's compensation package provide the Head with reasonable career predictability. Provide the support the Head needs in a position that demands responsibility, yet can be lonely and isolating.

The paradox is that while the Head is the Board's only employee, the Board is (as an entity) unable or incompetent to evaluate the totality of the Head's position and places its relationship at risk should it attempt this. Boards will exacerbate this problem by making the evaluation process a formality—filling out a form once a year and having a meaningless conversation with the Head through the Board President.

Instead, set up a Board committee (the Head Support and Evaluation Committee) to implement the evaluation function and ensure the contract includes this provision, with the attendant details. This group forms a relationship with the Head that:

- focuses on providing the resources needed (expert advice, dollars, time, professional development);
- holds the Head accountable; and
- ensures there are no surprises at contract-renewal time—either for or against the renewal.

The relationship between the Head and the Board should be predictable, supportive, and reciprocal. Use the Head contract to describe, enhance, and build a strong partnership.

An Annotated School Head Contract

This model has been prepared to fit contract renewal for an experienced Head, but it can be readily adapted for other circumstances. With a newly employed Head, all terms that refer to continuance would not be used in the initial contract, nor would a school be likely to provide for a minisabbatical as specified in Promise 9. The model also provides for school housing (Promise 5) and a school vehicle (Promise 7)—both easily omitted.

These types of agreements are, in general, governed by the laws of the state where the school is located. Because these laws may differ, it is important that you have your legal advisor review all contracts. This model contract is not considered copyrighted material. Copy this contract and adapt it to your school's needs. Be sure to have your school's lawyer review it and ensure it meets all state regulations.

Contract Provisions

This agreement is made as of _____ (month/day/year) between _____ ("School") and _____ ("Head").

Background

A. Head is currently employed in that capacity by School under an agreement.

B. Head and School desire to enter into a new form of agreement governing all aspects of Head's further employment.

C. Head is not under other contractual obligations.

Promises

In consideration of the mutual promises set forth herein, it is hereby agreed as follows:

1. All agreements heretofore entered by the parties bearing upon Head's employment by School are hereby rescinded, so as to be of no force and effect following the signing of this new agreement.

   This provides a clean slate, but any provisions of the preceding contract can be easily repeated.

2. School shall continue with Head in his present employment until June 30 [of the following academic year], on the terms and conditions hereinafter set forth. The contract is a two-year, rolling contract to be issued every 12 months. There is no expectation or guarantee of contract renewal; this is at the Board's discretion.

   In short, the new contract supersedes the remainder of the old one and continues through another academic year. The contract is a two-year, rolling contract renewed annually.

3. Head shall remain the Chief Executive Officer of School and the official advisor and executive agent of the Board of Trustees and its Executive Committee. In this employment, the Head performs all tasks necessary and appropriate to be done as Head, and shall be bound by all the rules and regulations heretofore or hereafter prescribed by the Board of Trustees, and will meet all requirements of such Board.

   The Head is empowered to sign contracts with others on behalf of the Board and the school, yet the Head is held to policies formally established by the Board.

4. School will compensate Head for services through June 30 [the current academic year], at the annual rate of $_____$, payable in equal monthly installments on the last day of each month, and will thereafter compensate Head at the annual rate of $_____$, also payable in monthly installments on the last day of each month through June 30 [the next academic year].

This allows the current salary to be continued or, hopefully, a higher salary to be set. (Remember, it is the Head who negotiates salary increases with subordinates; it is only fair that the Head and the Board go through the same process beforehand.)

5. Head and Head's family shall reside in the house provided by School for the use of Head in order that Head may effectively perform prescribed duties. Head's occupation of the residence is a condition of employment by School. As a representative of School, Head will use said house for meetings of students, faculty, staff, alumni, visiting teachers, scholars, and speakers, and for such other School functions and affairs as shall be appropriate for the best interest and development of School. Head shall occupy the property without payment of rent, and School will pay all cost of maintenance of the house and grounds. School at its sole cost and expense will furnish heat, light, and water, and will pay the cost of any sewer charges and garbage collection. Any taxes which may be assessed against the Head's house will be paid by School. Head shall pay for telephone service, but all toll charges or calls made in connection with School business shall be charged to or paid by School.

By making the use of school housing a necessary condition of employment and execution of the job, the IRS accepts this "employee benefit" as tax exempt—as long as the residence is on school property, immediately adjacent, or between two campuses. The Head should ensure that the residence is indeed used for the purposes set forth in the contract; otherwise, the IRS may not allow the benefit as tax exempt.

6. Reasonable and necessary expenses incurred by Head in connection with School business will be prepaid or reimbursed from School funds allocated for this purpose. These include, but are not limited to, travel, meals, lodging while away from School, dues for professional organizations, necessary gift and entertainment expenses, general housekeeping expenses incurred in the operation of the residence. All such payments shall be subject to such limitations and conditions as the Board of Trustees may impose from time to time.

Some schools arrange to reimburse the Head on a "per person" scale for hosting at the residence, if the school does not pay the direct cost of personnel and provisions. Thus, a separate letter of understanding would set amounts for lunches, dinners, formal dinners, and all other kinds of occasions.

7. School shall furnish to Head a car, together with the cost of maintaining, repairing, operating, and insuring the same for the use of Head in performing school-related duties. The car is available for personal use, subject to proper tax adjustments.

   A system should be determined with input from the school's attorney and accountant. Factors such as the type of car and how much it is used for business or personal use will influence whether the Head reimburses the school for personal use or the school adds that information to a W-2 as taxable income.

8. Head shall continue to be entitled to four weeks of vacation per year, plus _____ personal days, provided, however, that the time of such vacation or personal time off shall be approved by an officer of the Board and shall not interfere with the operation of School program.

   Allowance is thus made for the Head to take leave during school vacations and, as the job allows, during school operation. In many circumstances, a school is well-served by a Head who remains on duty during most of the summer to fill in as various administrators take vacations. The Head then goes on leave during the year when all administrators are available to cover the Head's responsibilities collectively.

9. School recognizes that Head can best serve School as a professionally productive and active leader in the field of private education. School, therefore, agrees that, in lieu of a sabbatical, Head may elect to spend up to 20 work days each year in private study, writing, or travel related to such education. Head is to receive full and regular compensation during such times, but dates are to be selected so as not to interfere with the operation of School program.

   This is designed to encourage professional refreshment and growth. It should not be confused with time spent representing the school at professional gatherings such as association meetings. It is a benefit that pays dividends to the school as well as the Head.

10. Head shall be entitled to _____ (dollars or units) of life insurance to be paid by School. In addition, Head is entitled to participation in all employee benefits accorded to professional personnel of School, as governed by the eligibility and administrative criteria and regulations of each plan.

    In rewriting this promise to fit your school and environment, don't fail to include other employee benefits that may be unique to the needs of your Head—such as child care services, club membership, or the use of other school-owned property. Additional life insurance, long-term disability, long-term care, and other benefits can be added. However, participation is limited to the conditions and restrictions of each plan.

11. Head shall be evaluated by the Head Support and Evaluation Committee (HSEC). Criteria for evaluation shall be derived from the strategic plan and annual administration agenda. The HSEC will meet to continually access progress of, and provide support and resources for, Head. The HSEC will recommend (or not) contract renewal.

    The Board commits to a strategic approach to planning that ripples into all evaluation processes in the school (and at the Board level). The Head is assessed against no more than six significant objectives, which will be "difference-makers" at the school. Other obligations of the Head are considered due diligence.

12. Upon recommendation of contract renewal, the Board will negotiate the compensation factors for the next year of Head's rolling contract.

    The Board approves the compensation package as a whole.

13. In the event that the Board requires at its sole discretion that Head cease to perform his duties before the conclusion of this contract, it is agreed that the first _____ of the remaining months will be paid at the full applicable salary, and that the months remaining in the contract thereafter will be compensated at one-third the applicable salary. It is further agreed that all forms of employee benefits including housing [and food] will be directly provided throughout the active contract, or a fair market monetary equivalent will be paid monthly at the sole discretion of the Board. School also agrees to pay travel and household moving expenses incurred by Head and his family upon departure—up to a distance equal to that incurred by Head upon initial employment by School. (The provisions of this section shall be voided one month after active employment is commenced elsewhere.)

14. In the event Head breaches this agreement or is terminated for cause (including but not limited to gross misconduct, insubordination, failure to perform), School, in addition to all other applicable remedies, may cease all forms of compensation immediately. The parties agree that calculation of actual damages to School would be extremely difficult and therefore agree that an amount of $_____ per day, for the remaining days of the contract, will be payable to School by Head as liquidated damages.

15. Head agrees to inform, within two weeks, the President of the Board, or another Board officer in the event of the president's unavailability, of any contact with anyone acting in the capacity of a Head search for another school. The Board agrees that it will not take any action injurious to Head as a result of such notification.

16. Head is free to submit a resignation effective at the end of this contract and at any time before the execution of a new contract that supercedes this agreement. The Board agrees that it will not take any action injurious to Head as a result of such a resignation.

Promises 13–16 cover conditions of separation. The pay-out provision should be negotiable with the Head. The Board should allow the Head to announce intentions of leaving well in advance of separation, without penalty. The Head should be able to notify the Board when he is in contact with another school before resignation, whether or not there is any intent to pursue the possibility of a new position.

17. The Board of Trustees recognizes that support of the position held by Head is essential to the smooth and effective operation of School, and it agrees it will exercise its best efforts to convey such support publicly.

This is a provision that may be hard to enforce, but it emphasizes the need for a Board to keep its confidences—particularly any individual or collective opinions of the Head and his performance.

In witness whereof, the parties hereto have caused this agreement to be duly executed. This represents the full agreement of both parties, and any verbal promises are not valid. If any one provision of the contract is deemed invalid, all other contractual provisions remain valid.

Sealed and delivered in the presence of: Signatures of Board President and Head

_____

Support and Evaluation of the School Head

The Head Support and Evaluation Committee links the school's planning document (and Board agenda) to the School Head's plan. Once it is clear what the Head is being asked to do for the coming year, the question the committee must ask is: How can we support the Head to ensure success and thus the continued strategic motion of the school?

It would be easy to focus on meeting regularly with the Head to assess progress toward achieving agreed-on objectives, while ignoring the developmental needs the Head may have in one or more of the objectives identified. It is likely that each year will present the Head with challenging assignments.

However, the Head is isolated at the top of the school's administration (in terms of responsibility for all aspects of the school's operations and in terms of being the Board's only employee). He or she needs a support team to ensure the challenges are met well and result in creative growth of the individual and of the school. This team, the HSEC, ensures the Head's oppportunities to learn and develop as the school's leader will occur over time (i.e., continually, as a process), assuring increasing effectiveness both of the Head and of the school. An important consideration from the Head's viewpoint: This process is a "safe" one, allowing the Head to admit to developmental needs without career risk.

Note here that development of the individual is not equivalent to sending the Head to a number of courses. While training off the job should not be undervalued, place a greater emphasis on development that occurs within the context of the Head's own work. Challenging assignments, approached appropriately, become positive learning experiences. Relationships with both Trustees and Leadership Team members offer similar opportunities for growth. Thus, consider the Head's development as multidimensional, enabling the Head to cope with steep learning curves within an environment that is not entirely predictable.

Consider using a mix of the following methods for support. Ensure the first method (assessment) is part of any approach you choose.

1. **Assessment:** Identifying the gap between the skills possessed and the skills needed to fulfill the agenda items is a critical step before establishing a professional development plan for any given year. Various methods and tools can be accessed to enable the Head to gain greater self-knowledge. The HSEC's role is to link the feedback proactively to the Head's action plan. Information of this kind is not to be used for evaluative purposes (in the traditional, negative sense). Such use will inhibit openness and a willingness to learn.

- Self-assessment is part of the process whereby the Head can form an accurate picture of herself or himself.
- In-process assessment by the HSEC, particularly once the relationship is developed well, can provide formal and informal feedback to the Head.
- In-process 360-degree feedback offers a formal way for the Head to gain understanding of his or her impact on direct reports and the Board, and can be done either internally or through an outside agency.
- Study of books enables the Head to keep up to date with current research and to maintain a broad knowledge and interests that will inform good decision-making. (Consider *Good Business* by Mihaly Csikszentmihalyi, *Professional Communities and the Work of High School Teaching* by Milbrey McLaughlin, or *The Human Side of School Change* by Robert Evans.)
- Use of journals such as *Educational Leadership* or the *Harvard Business Review* accomplishes the same goals as the study of books.
- Conversation with family and friends offers insight into personal development from a direction that can, at times, be far more revealing and even honest than conversation with one's professional colleagues.
- Previous feedback from performance reviews enables the Head to maintain perspective as to advances made (and encouragement about those advances!) and the need to recognize that development is a journey or process, not an event.

2. **Resources:** Given the strategic objectives the Board wants to accomplish are in themselves developmental (as challenging assignments), the HSEC should ensure that sufficient resources have been provided to the Head to accomplish them. This might be in the form of:
   - adequate office personnel to handle the administrative work;
   - experienced administrators to whom the Head can delegate responsibilities to free up time; or
   - simply the money to carry out the task, whether it is, for example, professional entertainment funds when soliciting donors or funds to print materials.

3. **Balance:** The committee cannot "coerce" balance between the Head's school work and commitments to family and community. The committee can, however, include the issue in the regular meeting conversations and show care and concern that these areas of life are being kept in balance.

4. **Failure strategies:** The HSEC can clearly work with the Head to recognize the possibility of failure and to deal with failure through:
    - anticipation by continuously evaluating and re-evaluating progress,
    - aid in reprioritization of agenda items to focus on those that are proving more troublesome;
    - provision of additional resources;
    - provision for specific training; and
    - reflection on the failure, if it occurs, to ensure that learning results, and any mistakes made are not repeated by either the Head or the Board.

5. **Reflection:** The HSEC, with the Head, can use the following simple questions to look at how an action or series of actions can be used for learning purposes.
    - What happened? Is there evidence? Of what quality is the evidence?
    - What did we learn (good or bad)?

6. **Mentoring:** Members of the committee can provide powerful advice, given their own self-knowledge of skills, experiences, and preferences.

7. **Coaching:** With any given item, the Head might be provided with a coach to walk through the process. Depending on the needs identified, this person might be a member of his or her own Leadership Team (e.g., the Development Director), a Board member, a professional coach, or a knowledgeable and skillful friend.

8. **Training:** Targeted training is another avenue through workshops, seminars, and the like.

As a member of the HSEC, keep two important principles in mind as you engage with the Head this year.
- Developmental training is a process, not an event.
- The Head's challenges require a mix of methods that will change over time.

The goal of the support provided by the Head Support and Evaluation Committee is to ensure there is a fit between the skills, perspectives, and competencies the Head has and the challenges that he or she has been charged with meeting. Effective use of the methods outlined above ensure the Head continues to develop in the areas that best benefit the future of the school and him or herself.

Maintain a Complete and Accurate Head's File

With any employer-employee relationship, your school must maintain paper and electronic files. Just as your school should have a policy on what is contained in an employee's file and who will keep it, your Board must do the same for its sole employee—the School Head. Basic documents on payroll and benefits should be kept by the Business Office. However, the Head's contracts, evaluations, and supporting documents (and other employment-related correspondence) should not be accessible to anyone in the school. Only the Board should see this confidential information. (Access to health records should be limited even further—perhaps only to the Board President.)

If the Head has many years of service at the school, over time the file may become fragmented. With turnover of the Board (and its leadership), parts of the Head's file may reside with one or more Board Presidents or the school's attorney. The "corporate memory" may become fuzzy, concentrating only on the moment and losing track of the Head's accomplishments in previous years. For the benefit of the Head and the Board, address this issue—with legal counsel guidance.

In these contentious times, if a Board and School Head become embroiled in a lawsuit, the Head's personnel file can be subpoenaed. This applies whether the issue is between the Board and the School Head, or involves a third party—such as a student, parent, or government agency—making claims against the school. If the information is split among several different files, each of these partial files can be subject to subpoena, and, thus, discovery in court.

The complete file should contain substantiated documents and information. All content should be as specific and objective as possible (e.g., employment contracts, annual reviews, and supporting documents). Following this rule, review of the file by any party (e.g., attorney or court) should be noncontroversial and without drama—no "smoking-gun" surprises.

Charge the Head Support and Evaluation Committee with keeping and maintaining the Head's file. With legal guidance, establish a systematic procedure for purging it of unnecessary documents and for turning over the file (when the person charged with its keeping, typically the HSEC Chair, is succeeded). Given the file should not be visible to any school employee, and because of Board turnover issues, the school's attorney should keep appropriate control of file access. Documents for inclusion in the file would be forwarded securely from the HSEC Chair to the attorney.

The Board, in consultation with the Head, must make clear the limited access to the file, designating those few individuals who have authority over the file. This typically includes the Board President, the HSEC Chair, and the school attorney. In fact, it's a good idea to incorporate the access agreement in the Head's contract to eliminate different interpretations of the procedure.

The File for the Departing School Head

Before the Head leaves the school, the Chair of the HSEC should meet with him or her to review the file. Assuming no current legal action exists where the file's content may be germane, the HSEC Chair decides on what remains in the file. In the case of a difference of opinion, appeal to the Board President, whose decision is final. Consult with the school's legal counsel to ensure the decision conforms to appropriate legal statutes.

After finalizing the contents, seal and store the departing Head's file—perhaps in a safe-deposit box or a locked drawer in the school's safe (if one exists). The Board should provide a copy to the school's legal counsel so there is a back-up memory should a significant amount of time pass before it is needed again.

Establish a policy about your Head's file now, when it is not an item of controversy or being subpoenaed. The Board can then be secure in the knowledge that all pertinent information and documents are handled in a responsible and secure manner, protecting everyone concerned.

CHAPTER TWELVE

The Board's Role in Fundraising

The central philanthropic duty of Trustees—each member's personal involvement in giving to the school and securing resources from others—is often unclear to Trustees, particularly those members who are new to the Board. ISM frequently hears comments like the following.

- "What is the Board's role in giving and raising money?"
- "We know what the Board's overall role is, but our Trustees don't recognize their own responsibilities."
- "When I was asked to join the Board, it was never made clear to me that I would have to make a gift, much less that I would have to ask others for money."
- "I give time and therefore shouldn't be expected to give money."

How do you make sure such miscommunication or lack of understanding doesn't happen on your Board?

A properly profiled Board is one step toward communicating philanthropic responsibilities. Board profiling is driven by your school's planning documents—the strategic plan and strategic financial plan. The strategic financial plan provides the fiscal resources to operate the strategic plan. Your Trustees also provide financial support through their giving. Your Committee on Trustees should make these responsibilities clear during the recruitment process and again during new-Trustee orientation. Ongoing professional development of Trustees, and the Development Director attending Board meetings and related committee meetings, can assist in these efforts as well.

A Board that robustly embraces its philanthropic responsibilities empowers your school to realize its goals and dreams. Board philanthropy is fueled by how well each Trustee knows and can define your school's institutional purposes in ways that are visionary and practical. That is not enough, however.

An enthusiastic Trustee who has a clear picture of your school's students and faculty, mission, priorities, and funding needs will assume the following duties.

- The Trustee contributes to the fullest measure within his or her means to annual, capital, and endowment campaigns, and the major gifts program.
- The Trustee sets the standard of giving for others with his or her own contribution.
- The Trustee is involved in identifying, engaging, evaluating, recognizing, and stewarding major gift prospects and donors. Examples of effective involvement include:
  - identifying individuals to bring them closer to your school;
  - annually cultivating and stewarding a portfolio of donors. Good examples of this include updating donors who have already given, reminding them that their gift made a difference, and inviting them to those programs and activities that match their values and interests;
  - introducing donors to other solicitation team members during visits;
  - writing follow-up and acknowledgment letters; and
  - hosting small gatherings.
- The Trustee serves in leadership roles, which may include becoming a:
  - Chair of the Annual Fund Cabinet or a Chair of one of its divisions (Leadership, Parents, Alumni, Faculty, or Staff);
  - Chair or member of the Development Committee; or
  - Chair or member of the Major Gifts Committee.

- The Trustee serves on solicitation teams either as solicitor, educator, or cultivator.
- The Trustee offers testimony, including:
  - being featured in your school's annual report or magazine, and
  - hosting parlor meetings or dinner dialogues.
- The Trustee identifies potential Board candidates.

Donors and prospects look to the Board for leadership when considering their own gifts. The philanthropic commitment of your Board helps to create the culture of philanthropy in your school and leads fundraising efforts for your internal and external constituencies.

The Board's Role in the Annual Fund

Your Trustees are the champions of all your fundraising efforts, through their leadership roles in campaigns as well as their own financial support. The development professionals, School Head, and volunteer development leaders, know the annual fund is one of your most important fundraising programs. The annual fund provides the platform for developing a culture of philanthropy at your school. Trustees are the school's volunteer leaders and fiduciary stewards, and therefore play a pivotal role in ensuring that your annual campaign achieves its goals.

Your annual fund keeps the mission at the forefront for donors and prospects each year, providing ongoing opportunities for your school community to fund program enhancements. This is where you can count on predictable, renewed support from the largest number of donors and prospects. The annual fund instills a habit of giving, and is when your major donors often make their initial gift. Board members have several responsibilities, collectively and individually, during every annual campaign.

1. **Trustees must be the first to give.** In every campaign, individual Board members must be the first to make a gift. Your school cannot expect others to give if the Board is not "all in." Before any public announcement of the campaign, 100% of the Board should already have made a commitment. This solidarity demonstrates faith in the campaign, and support for the school, and sets an example for all other donors.

   Taking the lead means giving generously within each individual's capacity. The message from the Board's leadership is clear: "As Trustees, we see the school as one of our top philanthropic activities. We donate to every campaign, and give to the fullest extent of our capabilities." On this last point, let the phrase "give until it feels good" be your guide.

The viability and stability of your school rests with your Trustees and their understanding of their strategic and philanthropic roles. Donors and prospects want to know that your Trustees gave, inspiring them to give themselves. When Trustees do not support the annual fund fully and enthusiastically, other donors will not give—or will give only nominally. The philanthropic commitment of your Board helps to create the culture of philanthropy in your school, and leads fundraising efforts for your internal and external constituencies.

2. **Trustees must actively engage in at least one area of the Donor Cycle.** This is as true of the annual fund as of any campaigns to support the school. They can identify individuals who would enjoy participating in the annual campaign, and cultivate potential donors by updating them about what is going on at the school or hosting small gatherings. They can help to solicit by serving as one of the constituency Chairs of the annual fund and by making appeals either in person or by letter. They can engage in recognition and stewardship by thanking annual fund donors and celebrating the success of the campaign.

3. **Trustees must approve the campign goals.** The Board must determine how much will be raised and how the money will be spent. This support must rest on a foundation of knowledge. Fully inform individual Trustees about the ways the campaign will enhance the school's programs and the attendant benefits to students. Bearing the responsibility for setting school policies and procedures, the Board, led by its Development Committee, is ultimately responsible for determining campaign goals. Set a reasonable strategy with ambitious goals that reflect a continued commitment to grow the campaign, increasing the dollar goal and strengthening participation among various constituencies. Always base such goals on data-guided discussions.

4. **The Board should avoid using the annual fund to fill budget gaps.** The Board's fiduciary responsibility is to define annual fund objectives to achieve program enhancements rather than to fill budgetary gaps. The school's regular operating expenses should be covered by "hard income"—tuition and fees, as determined by your strategic financial plan. Your plan needs to fund your mission. Funding budgetary gaps through your annual fund is neither sustainable nor a compelling reason for individuals to invest in your school. People engaged with your school want to give—even more so when the school is "winning" through program enhancements rather than struggling to cover expenses.

5. **The Board must provide resources.** For your Trustees to succeed, they need to be able to rely on a strong and skilled development team. The Board must ensure through the strategic plan that the Development Office has the financial and human resources required to support and coordinate the contributions of the Board to fundraising efforts. The development team needs the resources and talent that are necessary to conduct all the essential functions of the campaign, including:
    – creating and implementing a strategic plan for the annual fund;
    – gathering and communicating information about the projects to be funded;
    – collecting and tracking financial data and ensuring accuracy of the donor database;
    – supporting the Trustees by providing needed orientation and coaching;
    – providing logistical support in all phases of the donor cycle;
    – ensuring all the right steps in the process are completed in the right order; and
    – recording and acknowledging gifts.

There are costs for recruiting and retaining mission-focused, ambitious professionals who energize and support your Trustees. These professionals must also be provided with the funds they need to carry out their respective duties. The Board must collaborate with the School Head to determine what resources are required and ensure they are incorporated into your strategic financial plan.

The success of any campaign is proportionate to the Board's commitment. A Board that embraces its philanthropic responsibilities empowers its school to realize its goals. The Board sets the pace, and donors look to the Board to determine their own level of interest. The Board President, Development Committee, and Committee on Trustees should emphasize these duties to the entire Board before embarking on each year's annual fund drive. Determine how to deliver this important message so that fulfilling these responsibilities becomes an ingrained and integral part of the Board's culture.

The Board's Role in a Capital Campaign

A capital campaign grounded in the Board's understanding of (and commitment to) its strategic role is critical for campaign success. The following four core elements are critical to institutional readiness as the Board considers embarking on a capital campaign.

1. Strategic Planning and Strategic Financial Planning

Schools may raise money without a strategic plan and strategic financial plan, but school campaigns anchored in strong planning documents are far better positioned to raise inspirational money. Savvy donors view their philanthropic gifts as community investments. They want to know how the school budgets for the campaign and how the funds raised advance strategic objectives.

These plans set forth strategic objectives related to money, organizational structure, technology, facilities and grounds, and the school's position in the marketplace. Associated with each objective are cost estimates, expected implementation strategies sequenced by year, and those responsible for carrying out each objective. A plan that includes your capital campaign provides the Board, School Head, Leadership Team, and campaign leadership with a snapshot of all revenue sources—operations budget, campaign budget and revenues, and cash reserves—for each item.

There are advantages when your strategic plan funds campaign costs such as a campaign feasibility study and fundraising counsel from the operating budget. Use hard income or cash reserves instead of recouping costs from campaign revenues. This allows flexibility to sequence a "payment plan" for these costs spread over a number of years. And it often motivates donors and prospects to give when they see their campaign gifts going directly and entirely to programs or buildings.

2. Annual Board and Administration Agendas

The annual Board and administration agendas keep your strategic plan in motion, track the various tasks, and clarify the Board's and Head's responsibilities. The same holds true when embarking on a capital campaign.

Annual Board agenda: This agenda consists of Board-related strategic plan items for the upcoming year. Each item may have several associated tasks.

Annual administration agenda: The School Head creates an administrative agenda following the same process summarized above for the Board. The Head delegates the execution of the agenda items to Leadership Team members as appropriate. For example, since one of the items above is to identify top gift prospects for the campaign, that task would be assigned to the Development Director.

3. Board Profiling and the Committee on Trustees

A profiled Board helps ensure the success of a campaign. Profiling the Board is the job of the Committee on Trustees (see Chapter Nine), and is a process with specificity. The question the Committee on Trustees must ask is: To enable the school to execute its strategic plan and strategic financial plan with the greatest distinction, what mix of characteristics is required of the Trustees? Failure to recruit strategically may result in a group of people who, while enthusiastic about the school, are unable to forward the school vision.

The Committee on Trustees needs to plan early to ensure school support during the feasibility study and when launching the quiet phase of the campaign. With this in mind, the committee might identify the need for:

- ongoing education of Board candidates on the campaign;
- three major donors on the Board to make gifts at the leadership level;
- cultivation of candidates to serve in campaign leadership positions; and
- two (or more) passionate advocates for the school on the Board who have high community profiles.

While it is the Committee on Trustees' job to profile and cultivate new Board members, the Development Committee and Major Gifts Committee are invaluable in helping to create a slate of candidates. Excellent communication among these three committees ensures that cultivation efforts are coordinated. When in campaign mode, consider the following suggestions.

- Schedule a meeting with the committee Chairs before every Board meeting to discuss cultivation of prospects and enlist the help of other Trustees as appropriate. Provide a summary report to the Board.
- Schedule formal joint meetings among the three committees to share knowledge, discuss strategy, and assign responsibility.
- Identify a common member of all three committees to update the Committee on Trustees.

4. Board Leadership and Ongoing Trustee Education

The success of any capital campaign is proportionate to the Board's commitment. Trustees provide financial support through their giving. Your Committee on Trustees should make these responsibilities clear during the recruitment process and Trustee orientation.

A Board that embraces its philanthropic responsibilities empowers your school to realize its goals and dreams when embarking on a campaign. The Board sets the campaign's pace, and donors look to the Board to determine the interest. It is critical that Trustees:

- understand and be able to advocate for the school's mission;

- unanimously accept the campaign goals;
- be willing to fulfill appropriate duties assigned by the campaign leadership;
- recognize and accept the considerable commitment of time and energy required of them;
- have in their membership those with sufficient means and access to means to carry the lion's share of the campaigns leadership phase;
- ensure that 100% of the Board participate financially, each member to his or her potential. Trustees must recognize that they are responsible for bringing in at least 25% of the goal—and preferably 30%;
- be involved in identifying, engaging, evaluating, soliciting, recognizing, and stewarding all levels of gift prospects and donors; and
- serve on solicitation teams, either as solicitor, educator, or cultivator.

Many private schools, regardless of size or age, embark on capital campaigns. With an increasingly competitive philanthropic environment, the Board must fulfill its roles and responsibilities in fortifying a school's institutional readiness to launch a campaign. Readiness to embrace a campaign, to inspire donors to give, and to ensure success is greatly enhanced when your school commits to:

- strategic planning and strategic financial planning;
- annual Board and administrative agendas;
- Board profiling and a Committee on Trustees; and
- Board leadership and ongoing Trustee education.

The greater the Board's ability to fulfill its strategic role (as represented by these activities), the more inspired other volunteer leaders will be to join ranks. The partnership with the School Head and the Leadership Team becomes stronger as well. With this support, the Head has the Board's commitment to provide the resources needed—and, ultimately, for the faculty to deliver the school's mission to its students.

The Strategic Board and the Advancement Model

When you look at the Comprehensive Advancement Model developed by ISM, "Strategic Board" forms the base. Simply stated, the effectiveness of your advancement program is inextricably linked to your school's overall stability, and the Board is the guarantor of stability. When the Board operates strategically—focusing on sustaining financial viability and excellence for future generations of students—every aspect of school operations performs at a higher level, including advancement efforts.

ISM Comprehensive Advancement Model

The Board's strategic plan and strategic financial plan serve as the guide for maintaining the school's viability and stability. When advancement goals are incorporated into the plan, they become components of that strategic operation—they are defined, put on a time line, costed out, and assigned to a specific group or individual. The "Strategic Board" foundation creates optimal conditions for carrying out the components of the advancement model—Enrollment Management, Development, and Marketing Communications.

- **Enrollment Management:** Strategic Boards provide the resources to deliver the mission with excellence and provide faculty professional growth. This supports admission's efforts to successfully recruit and re-recruit mission-appropriate students as expert faculty deliver on the mission's promise.

- **Development:** The strategic plans, with the strategic Board standing behind them, inspire confidence and provide a powerful case for motivating donors. Donors are proud to give and get involved. They view their philanthropic gifts as investments in their own children, the school community, and the future these students will create.

- **Marketing Communications:** The strategic Board and plans demonstrate how the school lives its mission, and contribute to developing the school's unique message, which will serve as the central theme of both internal and external marketing.

The "Strategic Board" also forms the base of the advancement model because of the essential roles the Board plays in supporting the full range of advancement efforts. As school ambassadors, Trustees offer testimony about their own experiences. They talk about why they embrace their trusteeship; why they select your school, year after year, for their own children; and why they continue to give to your school's various fundraising programs. They tell the school's story, spreading the word about its values, accomplishments, future, and impact on the community.

Boards that sustain a "strategic focus" on advancement typically have the following characteristics.

- The Board incorporates advancement goals in its strategic plan and strategic financial plan.
- Board members serve as the "first wave" of donors for each fundraising effort and give to capacity. The school should be able to say that 100% of its Trustees contribute to a campaign.
- Board members receive ongoing education about advancement to help them understand and carry out crucial leadership roles.
- The Trustees have a clear understanding of the school's mission, values, benefits, and programs, and can talk effectively about them.
- The Board periodically examines the school's mission and marketplace niche and stance to ensure the school distinguishes itself from its competitors.

Having a strategic Board as the foundation of your advancement efforts clearly provides the best possible approach for success.

Strategic Board Assessment

Historically, evaluation of the Board of Trustees has been either (a) nonexistent or (b) accomplished via a generic form designed for use by any nonprofit Board. If the results were used at all, they formed the basis for a discussion at an annual retreat session. This exercise is best described as corporate self-analysis that seldom leads to diagnosis and prescription for reconfiguring Board structure and function (i.e., for Board development) over time.

The responsibility for Board evaluation should lodge with the Committee on Trustees. The strategic Board ranks as ISM's No. 2 Stability Marker, second only to a school's mix of cash reserves, debt, and endowment. The Board unit responsible for determining the composition of the Board and the quality—the "strategic-ness"—of its structure and function, becomes the Board's most important unit in determining the long-term success of the school. This comprises the reason-for-being for your Committee on Trustees.

Two Ingredients

The Committee on Trustees blends two ingredients within its annual Board evaluation cycle: (1) Board self-evaluation and (2) assessment of the Board's productivity and professionalism.

To accomplish the first, the Committee on Trustees presides over a twice-yearly administration of ISM's Strategic Board Assessment instrument. To accomplish the second, the committee "grades" the Board's progress vis-à-vis the objectives shown in its annual Board agenda. Pursuant to this second ingredient, the Committee on Trustees addresses:

– the effectiveness of the Board committees as measured against the charges given to them; and

– the professionalism of individual Trustees, particularly as measured against the "due diligence" item (No. 15) in the assessment instrument that is central to the Board self-evaluation.

The **Board self-evaluation** step is grounded in the assessment instrument, a 15-item questionnaire designed to be completed in a regular Board meeting—ideally, December and May. Following this exercise, the Committee on Trustees meets to tabulate results, determine the overall score, and attend to those items on which the Board's self-score was lowest. Those low-scored items, as suggested by the scoring system itself, should form the basis for the Committee on Trustees Board development plan, a subset of the school's big-picture, six-year strategic plan. Design the Board development plan to bring the Board's self-score up to the criterion level shown in ISM's Stability Markers. (See Chapter Five).

Consider the second ingredient, Committee on Trustees **assessment of the Board's productivity and professionalism.** This approach builds on the premise that the Board President annually selects from the strategic plan those items which, in the coming year, are the Board's responsibility to implement. This should be a twice-yearly process, preferably in December and May. In preparation for full-Board meetings in winter and spring, the Committee on Trustees systematically examines the Board's progress against the objectives articulated the previous summer in the annual Board agenda.

This will be primarily a judgment of Board committee progress, and will necessitate gathering data from committee Chairs systematically. However, as committee projects reach completion, come before the Board as proposals, and are—or are not—approved and incorporated into the life of the Board and school, these judgments require less data collection and more simple review of full-Board actions and decisions. Use a straightforward grading system to score the Board's productivity. For each objective written into the annual Board agenda, a letter grade of A, B, or I (Incomplete) may be awarded, with notations as needed.

Any grade below "A" implies a recommendation by the Committee on Trustees for enhancement. This can be simple and private (i.e., communicated only to the President), such as: "The Committee on Trustees recommends replacing the Chair of Committee x with committee member y, who has actually done most of the work to date." Or it may be complex and public, such as "Committee z has been awarded an 'I,' not because of lack of committee leadership, effort, or professionalism, but because of the difficulty or impossibility of gathering necessary data or of inducing needed action. The Committee on Trustees recommends the Board President aid the goal-development process to lend her influence and prestige to data collection and action inducement."

An important subset of this second ingredient deals with the professionalism of individual Trustees. This derives from the "due diligence" item (No. 15) in the Strategic Board Assessment instrument. Twice a year, the Committee on Trustees should review individual Board members' performance, typically reported by the committee Chairs. At times, this review should result in a memo of commendation to individuals whose performance and dedication have been exemplary. At other times, this review may result in a conversation with the President and a subsequent meeting with a problem Trustee.

Caveat

The Board President must consider the Board's readiness to operate in the fashion recommended above. Discuss the question with other Board leaders (especially the Chair of the Committee on Trustees, who will assume these tasks) and with the School Head. This approach shifts some organizational power away from the President. The ideal Board President becomes much more a "manager" of Board-level operations than a "corporate Board Chair," with all centralized power and control that has gone hand-in-glove with that title.

Administer ISM's Strategic Board Assessment instrument as the first step in getting a sense of your Board's readiness. In your annual Board summer retreat, discuss the self-score outcomes and consider the wisdom of moving in the direction implied. Understand that, unless your Board seems determined not to move in this direction, presidential leadership implies that you can and should provide the balance-tipping arguments in favor. When colleagues on the Board see the willingness of the President to share power in the ways implied by a strong Committee on Trustees, they are likely to mirror that enthusiasm.

The Strategic Board Assessment Instrument

The Board President or Chair of the Committee on Trustees should begin to use this instrument in your annual or twice-annual administration of the assessment. Use this as an independent measure of your Board's strategic orientation and as a critical self-scoring component in the ISM Stability Markers. The instrument's revised scoring system yields a single 24-point total. That total comprises your Board's score on the governance portion of the ISM Stability Markers.

Use this instrument, as soon as practical, to establish a fresh baseline for scoring the Strategic Board Assessment. In developing your Board's strategic orientation, place early emphasis with your Trustees on the items weighted most heavily in ISM's statistical analysis. These items have the greatest impact on your school's long-term strategic strength, i.e., items No.1 and 11, and, secondarily, items No. 2, 3, 4, 8, 9, and 15. The remaining items should still receive your attention. Make your Trustees aware that those items will impact your Board's ability to influence strategic excellence in a tertiary fashion. That is, changes for the better on these items are not going to result in direct, immediate impact on the school's stability. Instead, they will support improvement on the primary and secondary items.

The Strategic Board Assessment

Date/Year: _____

This instrument is designed to be completed by Trustees at least once a year. The Committee on Trustees normally administers and scores the instrument. The committee then includes an analysis of its tabulation as part of the annual (or twice-annual) Board self-evaluation.

For Boards just beginning to move toward the strategic Board, the initial self-score serves as the foundation for a Board development plan, fashioned by the Committee on Trustees for Board consideration.

Individual Trustees: Please circle a number to best represents your impression of your Board on each of the 15 items below.

1. Our Trustees focus on the strategic, long-term impact of issues and decisions.

   0   1   2   3   4
   Rarely   Always

2. We have developed a planning document that is simultaneously visionary, practical, and financially feasible.

    0   1   2   3   4

    No planning document   Exemplary planning document

3. Each spring-summer, we create our annual Board agenda using items derived explicitly from our planning document.

    0   1   2   3   4

    No planning document   Board agenda derived explicitly from planning document

4. Our Committee on Trustees creates Board profiles (a list of descriptors or characteristics aligned with the planning document) and cultivates potential Trustees with the profile as guide.

    0   1   2   3   4

    No profile   Thorough profile-specific cultivation

5. Our full-Board meetings are organized around one major action item on which a vote is taken or a consensus is reached during the meeting.

    0   1   2   3   4

    Meetings not organized on this basis   Meetings organized on this basis

6. "Current day-to-day events" discussions do not dominate our full-Board meetings.

    0   1   2   3   4

    Current events dominate   Strategic and long-range issues dominate

7. There is a Head Support and Evaluation Committee (HSEC), or its equivalent, which assists the Head, when appropriate, in handling "current events issues" and which is the only forum for Head evaluation.

    0   1   2   3   4

    No HSEC exists   HSEC operates effectively (handling "current events issues" and evaluation)

8. Our Board committees are given explicit charges each year.

0	1	2	3	4
No charges				Annual charges for all committees

9. Our Committee on Trustees evaluates the Board based on the Board's fulfillment of its annual Board agenda (which is, in turn, derived annually from the planning document), and the Board takes action.

0	1	2	3	4
No Committee on Trustees evaluation				Comprehensive formal evaluation followed by appropriate action

10. Our Board has instituted a major gifts program and committee in which potential major donors are continuously cultivated year after year, regardless of when (or if) the next campaign is scheduled to begin.

0	1	2	3	4
No major gifts program and committee				In place and effective major gifts program and committee

11. There is depth of leadership on our Board (i.e., a number of individuals whom one can readily imagine in the Board presidency or holding critical committee Chair positions).

0	1	2	3	4
No leadership depth				Great leadership depth

12. There is a high level of mutual trust between our Board and our School Head.

0	1	2	3	4
No level of mutual trust				Very high level of mutual trust

13. Our Board places great emphasis on its annual new-Trustee orientation and on its continuing education process.

0	1	2	3	4
No education of any kind				Great emphasis on orientation and on continuing education

14. Our Board committees regularly tap the expertise of non-Trustees, using them as committee members, committee guests, or unofficial "consultants."

0	1	2	3	4
No use of non-Trustees				Appropriate use of non-Trustees by Board committees

15. One-hundred percent of our Trustees take their "due diligence" seriously (i.e., preparation for meetings; on-time attendance at all meetings; full participation in meetings; personal financial contributions promptly made in support of all fundraising goals; serious commitment to the confidentiality of Board matters; enthusiastic support publicly for the school, its faculty, its Head, and each Trustee's own Board colleagues).

0	1	2	3	4
None				100% of our Trustees

Scoring: The Strategic Board Assessment generates 24 possible points in the scoring of the 147-point ISM Stability Marker array; the scoring approach shown below conforms to that number (i.e., 24 possible points).

1. Average the participants' scores for numbers 1 and 11; multiply by 4 (range 0–16).
2. Average the participants' scores for numbers 2, 3, 4, 8, 9, and 15; multiply by 2 (range 0–8).
3. Sum these two (range 0–24).
4. Do not include items 5, 6, 7, 10, 12, 13, and 14 in the tabulation.

The items just listed in No. 4 above are included because they represent good practice in operating a "strategic" Board of Trustees. Thus, the Committee on Trustees should include these seven items in its annual analysis of the Board's strategic orientation. (This would mean, for example, reporting to the Board on mean scores for items 5, 6, 7, 10, 12, 13, and 14, just as on items 1, 2, 3, 4, 8, 9, 11, and 15.)

The items listed in No. 4 do not, however, correlate strongly with the ISM Stability Marker outcomes and, thus, do not play a role in determining your school's score on the Stability Markers. Use only the items in No. 1 and 2 in computing your Board's self-score on the governance portion of the Stability Markers.

A Sample Board Commitment and Trustee Handbook

Being a member of the Board of Trustees for a private school is an honor. You are being asked to take into your care a school, the entire student body. The Board must ensure the education each student receives fulfills the school's mission, and that all students are nurtured and developed in directions that benefit them. You are going to carry out that care by providing support—resources—to the School Head. Your relationship to the school will determine whether your school will be successful in the long term.

Being a Board member is also somewhat puzzling. If you're like many Trustees, you're not sure how it happened. Maybe you were approached at a social event. Maybe another Board member had talked to you quite a while ago about it on the phone; you may even have forgotten the conversation. Maybe you were serving on a committee and this seemed the next logical step.

It's also most likely that you are the parent of a student at the school. This makes being a Trustee more complicated. After all, surely you have a right to advocate for your child, right? Being a Board member gives you rather more influence to do that. Other parents, in fact, talk to you about their issues as well, hoping that you can help influence the process. In Board discussions, you imagine the impact of your decisions on your children and on your family, particularly when it comes to setting tuition.

Whatever your circumstances, the following two considerations are key as we begin this exploration of what you do as a Trustee.

You are a volunteer. This means:

- this is not the only thing you do! Being a Trustee is probably no higher than four or five on your list of priorities. Your Board obligations are less important than, for example, being a family person, having a career, engaging in meaningful relationships, and so on); and
- the Board meets relatively infrequently—maybe 10 meetings a year of an average two hours' duration, i.e., about 20 hours. Now, this obviously doesn't include other responsibilities such as serving on a committee, attending events, and engaging in development activities. But the decision-making function the Board exercises is carried out within a very small band of time.

You believe in the mission of the school. If you are a parent, you have seen the power of the school's mission in the lives of your children. You have firsthand experience of faculty commitment and have at least an inkling of the challenges faced by the School Head and Leadership Team. If you are not a parent, you have a picture of what this school can do for children in the community in which you live, for society as a whole. You are agree with the mission and, without being myopic, you support the school unconditionally. You may know parents at the school and vicariously enjoy their children's successes.

These two key considerations—being a volunteer and believing in the mission— have enormous ramifications. It means that, whatever other roles you may play as a parent, committee member, donor and so on, your role as Trustee is fundamentally carried out in two ways. As a Trustee, you are to:

- support the mission; and
- act strategically (as a grandparent) to ensure the school is there for the next generation.

You don't have time to do anything else.

A Trustee Handbook

This handbook lays out systematically the best practices for this to happen. As you read each section, be aware of your own context, culture, setting, and history, and consider how you might best use these practices in your own school. Each section begins with a guiding principle. Follow this with a discussion, provided with the expectation that you and your Board consider it thoughtfully, potentially varying the practice but always maintaining the principle.

It is our hope and ambition that each Trustee who uses this handbook in a proactive, thoughtful way, will be an effective Board member. This can enable the Board to dynamically support, strategically lead, and wisely steward the school in its care, empowering its students, School Head, faculty, staff, and Leadership Team to carry out their roles with excellence and confidence.

We encourage you to use this handbook yearly to help clearly identify for yourself what you want to achieve as a Trustee. This supports you in measuring and providing feedback for yourself and for your colleagues on your accomplishments and ambitions for your years on the Board.

Section 1: Mission Comparisons

Instructions. This section invites you to be thoughtful, at least once per year, about the school's reason-for-being, your own reason-for-being in that context, and the congruence (or not) between the two.

School mission. Please write the school mission statement or, alternatively, phrases from the mission, philosophy, and core values on which you expect to concentrate most forcefully and thoughtfully in the upcoming school year.

_____
_____
_____
_____

Personal and professional mission. Write into the space below a concise summary of your own reason-for-being as a school Trustee.

_____
_____
_____
_____

Comparison and contrast. Examine the two statements above. With marginal notes, circles, arrows, or other indicators, highlight any especially congruent or incongruent ideas or phrases. Note below the possible impact of these items on your agenda for the upcoming school year.

Section 2: Trustee Self-Rating

Instructions: Self-ratings. Following is a list of Trustee leadership and management characteristics. Rate yourself on each of the 14 items. Nine represents the "high" end of the scale. Once you have gone through the items, use the comment section at the end to reflect on how you see your own performance and what you would like to emphasize in the coming year.

Don't take on more than two areas to work at improving. Chances are you won't do it. Pick your one or two items and decide what you want to do about them. For example, you may have scored yourself low on No. 1 (vigorously pursue my own professional growth …). Determine to make attending the summer Board retreat and the workshop offered in the fall a high priority. Or you may have scored yourself low on No. 4 (demonstrate strategic thinking and oppose "current-parent" thinking). Decide only to engage with agenda items at meetings in the future, rather than bringing up current affairs topics that are not part of the agenda.

As a Trustee for my school, I …

1. Vigorously pursue my own professional growth in being a Trustee and encourage my fellow Trustees to do the same

   1   2   3   4   5   6   7   8   9

2. Show respect for others regardless of their position in the organization

   1   2   3   4   5   6   7   8   9

3. Consistently display "muted charisma" (i.e., a "strong personality" dampened by humility)

   1   2   3   4   5   6   7   8   9

4. Demonstrate strategic thinking and oppose "current-parent" thinking

   1   2   3   4   5   6   7   8   9

5. Carry out my Trustee due diligence (meeting attendance, etc.)

   1   2   3   4   5   6   7   8   9

6. Am seen as being steeped in moral purpose, clarity, conviction, and integrity
   1   2   3   4   5   6   7   8   9

7. Am seen as student-centered
   1   2   3   4   5   6   7   8   9

8. Display predictability (i.e., display consistency in my responses to others)
   1   2   3   4   5   6   7   8   9

9. Display supportiveness (i.e., display the attitude of being on the side of the administration, faculty, and staff even when I am in disagreement)
   1   2   3   4   5   6   7   8   9

10. Give public, positive reinforcement consistently
    1   2   3   4   5   6   7   8   9

11. Give financially at the level that I know I am capable of whenever asked
    1   2   3   4   5   6   7   8   9

12. Am seen as being self-aware, and as being effective at self-management (i.e., I am seen as someone who both monitors his or her behaviors and then modifies those behaviors as appropriate to be organizationally effective and to remain physically and mentally healthy)
    1   2   3   4   5   6   7   8   9

13. Am seen as displaying an inspired and inspirational commitment to the school mission
    1   2   3   4   5   6   7   8   9

14. Carry out my committee duties conscientiously
    1   2   3   4   5   6   7   8   9

Comment section (Choose one or two items and plan what you will do to improve.) The Committee on Trustees will hold you accountable for this!

Item: _____

Plan: _____

_____

_____

_____

Item: _____

Plan: _____

_____

_____

_____

Note: If you are falling down on your duties in, for example, No. 14, the Committee on Trustees may encourage you to include that as one of your items.

Section 3: Trustee Leadership and Management Agenda

Instructions: Fill out this sheet. There is space for only two committees. Do not commit to more than two and preferably only one. You need to do your job at a level of excellence. You are a volunteer. Don't set the school up for disappointment. There is a success comment so that you can write down the level of success you and your committee achieved at the end of your process. At the end of each year, this sheet will become part of your Trustee file held by the Committee on Trustees.

Committee No. 1: _____

Committee charge: _____

_____

_____

My responsibilities: _____

_____

_____

Date the committee is due to make its recommendation for action: _____

Success comment: _____

_____

Signed: _____ Print Name: _____

Date: _____

Committee No. 2: _____

Committee charge: _____

_____

_____

My responsibilities: _____

_____

_____

Date the committee is due to make its recommendation for action: _____

Success comment: _____

_____

Signed: _____ Print Name: _____

Date: _____

Section 4: Revisions, Discussions, Comments

Instructions: Annotate during the year to ensure that there is regular feedback, collection of data, provision of support, modification as necessary, and discussion of issues surrounding this document.

The Student Experience Profile

In the 2010–11 school year, ISM conducted a research project, titled the ISM Student Experience Study (SES), that focused on student performance, satisfaction, and enthusiasm. The following was one of the instruments derived from the SES findings, and is designed to be administered directly to private school students, grades 5 and higher.

Summary of Research Method and Conclusions

Eight schools were engaged in early fall of the 2010–11 school year. The schools collectively provided the study with single-sex and coed contexts; with PK–5, PK–8, PK–12, 7–12, and 9–12 grade configurations; with religiously affiliated and secular missions; and with day and boarding environments. At each school, 16 students were invited to participate (eight from each of two grade levels except in the PK–5 school, in which all 16 were fifth-graders). Students were selected by school administrators to conform to ISM's requirements:

– four students from each academic quartile;

– eight boys and eight girls (except in the three single-sex schools); and

– no students likely to be intimidated by interviewers from outside the school community (i.e., by ISM data-collection personnel).

Students were interviewed in pairs, near the end of each grading period.

ISM developed an interview instrument designed to measure (a) student perception of "predictability and support" in the environment; (b) student satisfaction; and (c) student enthusiasm. (These were the three most critical findings—in their relationship to student performance and to one another—from the original six-year project.)

The following conclusions are drawn by ISM.

- Data on the specific ingredients associated with student-perceived predictability and support, student-reported satisfaction, and student-reported enthusiasm within the school environment should be collected and analyzed regularly (i.e., at least once annually) by those in faculty leadership positions via use of the Student Experience Profile.

- Data on the specific ingredients associated with faculty, administrative, and coaching impact on student performance, satisfaction, and enthusiasm should be collected and analyzed regularly (i.e., at least once annually and preferably seasonally) by those in faculty leadership positions via use of the Faculty Culture Profile.

Use of the ISM Student Experience Profile

Your school's results from the ISM Student Experience Profile should serve as one basis for ongoing professional-development-focused conversations with individual teachers and, as well, with whole-faculty groups and subgroups. (The youngest students interviewed in the recent study were fifth-graders; in the original study, third-graders. ISM grants blanket permission to alter the language of the items to make them more intelligible to students younger than fifth-graders. Note that such changes may render ISM's to-be-established norms unusable under such conditions.)

Administer the instrument systematically. For example, if you choose a minimalist schedule, you might administer the instrument to a stratified random sample in two grade levels, the same season of the year (e.g., every fall), every year. Or, if you are equipped to set up the instrument electronically, you might administer the instrument to all students—fifth grade and older—fall, winter, and spring, every year. In other words, the size of the sample you select is a practical matter, having to do with your capacity to score the instrument. While it is impossible to gather "too much" data, it is certainly possible to consume so much staff time that the costs begin to outweigh the benefits. Small samples, carefully selected, can yield strong, highly useful outcomes.

Scoring

To score the Student Experience Profile to make outcomes comparable to the ISM Student Experience Study's outcomes, break each student's scores into the three scales.

Scale	Items Included	Maximum Score
Predictability and Support	2, 4, 5, 8, 9, 11, 12 (item 2 reverse scored)	63 (9 scale-points x 7 items)
Satisfaction	1, 7, 10	27 (9 scale-points x 3 items)
Enthusiasm	1, 3, 6 (item 1 double scored)	27 (9 scale-points x 3 items)

Hand-scoring can be expected to take roughly one person-hour for each 20 students. Thus, under hand-scoring conditions, student samples of 60 or fewer are suggested. (This assumes that the hand-scoring would result in each student's scale-score totals being entered on an Excel spreadsheet, at which point means and correlations could be computed nearly instantaneously by the software.)

Overview

Use the Student Experience Profile and the Faculty Culture Profile in conjunction with each other. Since Part A of the Faculty Culture Profile is derived just as directly from the ISM Student Experience Study, as is the Student Experience Profile, it is likely that enhancing your faculty's scores on the faculty instrument will eventually be reflected in similarly enhanced scores on the student instrument.

The ISM Student Experience Profile

Your school's results from the ISM Student Experience Profile should serve as one basis for ongoing professional-development-focused conversations with individual teachers and, as well, with whole-faculty groups and subgroups. (Note: the youngest students interviewed in the recent study were fifth-graders; in the original study, third-graders. ISM grants blanket permission to alter the language of the items to make them more intelligible to very young students, while noting that such changes may render ISM's to-be-established norms unusable under such conditions.)

Circle only one number for each item. Consider only the most recent grading period in your responses.

1. I have very much looked forward to coming to school every day of this grading period.

   1   2   3   4   5   6   7   8   9

   Not true of me at all   Exactly true of me

2. I have not seen or heard of bullying—of anybody being "picked on" in any way at all—anywhere in our school during this grading period.

   1   2   3   4   5   6   7   8   9

   Absolutely no bullying   Bullying every day

3. I find that I am proud of my school, and proud to be part of such a school.

   1   2   3   4   5   6   7   8   9

   Not true of me at all   Exactly true of me

4. It has been obvious to me that my teachers really want me to do well—in school and out of school.

   1   2   3   4   5   6   7   8   9

   Not accurate at all   Fully Accurate

5. My teachers have worked every day at helping me become a better, more ethical person, regardless of the subject they are teaching (math, science, English, history, etc.).

1   2   3   4   5   6   7   8   9

Not accurate at all   Fully Accurate

6. I have been very excited about what I've been studying this grading period (the course material itself, not the teaching of the material).

1   2   3   4   5   6   7   8   9

No, zero excitement   Yes, tremendous excitement

7. I'm so satisfied with my school, I'd certainly want to come here, if my family and I could choose again.

1   2   3   4   5   6   7   8   9

No, absolutely not   Yes, certainly

8. Our assessments this grading period have covered exactly what my teachers said they would cover.

1   2   3   4   5   6   7   8   9

No, our teachers always   Yes, our tests covered exactly
    tried to trick us   what we were told to study

9. All the grades I received during this grading period—big assessments, quizzes, papers, etc.—were exactly the grades I think I actually earned—no higher
or lower.

1   2   3   4   5   6   7   8   9

Never the correct grade   Always the correct grade

10. I have been completely satisfied with our rules.

1   2   3   4   5   6   7   8   9

Terrible, stupid rules   Perfectly appropriate rules

11. Our teachers have enforced our rules (including the dress code) justly, fairly, consistently.

    1   2   3   4   5   6   7   8   9

Unfair or no enforcement   Fair, just enforcement

12. I have known exactly what to expect from my teachers, every day; I have known just how they will react to anything we say or do.

    1   2   3   4   5   6   7   8   9

Teaches moody   Teaches perfectly
and unpredictable   consistent every day

To score the Student Experience Profile to make outcomes comparable to this study's outcomes (Table I), break each student's scores into the three scales: Predictability and Support scale: items 2, 4, 5, 8, 9, 11, 12 (item 2 reverse scored); Satisfaction scale: items 1, 7, 10; Enthusiasm scale: items 1, 3, 6. (Item 1 is double-scored.) Thus, for a given student, the P/S scale's maximum score is 63 (9 x 7 items); the Satisfaction and Enthusiasm scales' maximum scores are 27 each (9 x 3 items). Hand-scoring can be expected to take roughly one person-hour for each 20 students. Thus, under hand-scoring conditions, student samples of 60 or fewer are suggested. (This assumes that the hand-scoring would result in each student's scale-score totals being entered on an Excel spreadsheet, at which point means and correlations could be computed nearly instantaneously by the software.)

237 | The Student Experience Profile

APPENDICES

The Faculty Culture Profile

In the 2010–11 school year, as detailed in the previous appendix, ISM conducted the ISM Student Experience Study. Of course, the research had major implications for teachers, and ISM developed the Faculty Culture Profile to address these findings.

We repeat the two major SES conclusions here.

- Data on the specific ingredients associated with student-perceived predictability and support, student-reported satisfaction, and student-reported enthusiasm within the school environment should be collected and analyzed regularly (i.e., at least once annually) by those in faculty leadership positions via use of the Student Experience Profile.

- Data on the specific ingredients associated with faculty, administrative, and coaching impact on student performance, satisfaction, and enthusiasm should be collected and analyzed regularly (i.e., at least once annually and preferably fall, winter, and spring) by those in faculty leadership positions via use of the following Faculty Culture Profile.

Use of the ISM Faculty Culture Profile

The ISM Faculty Culture Profile ties explicitly to the ISM Student Experience Profile. This faculty culture instrument links strongly, then, to the ISM findings in the Student Experience Study regarding student performance, student satisfaction, and student enthusiasm. Your own school's outcomes from the two instruments may profitably be considered companion pieces in your ongoing efforts to monitor the extent to which "predictability and support" conditions are present, and how strongly so, within your teaching and learning environment.

Administer the instrument in fall, winter, and spring, with an Evaluation Design Team of exemplary teachers implementing the instrument and assisting faculty leaders and administrators in interpreting the outcomes, item by item. Since ISM has found that seasonal fluctuations in any faculty's self-scores on these items are to be expected, meaningful analysis of scores must be multiyear, same-season-to-same-season. (For example, a middle school faculty's self-scores in one November can be compared to that middle school faculty's self-scores, item by item, the following November, the November after that, and so on.)

Scoring

The most useful approach to scoring the Faculty Culture Profile is not to calculate means and standard deviations, but to calculate the percentage of the faculty that scores each item at the "good end" of the scale. The Faculty Culture Profile uses a nine-point scale. Calculate the percent of the faculty that scores 7, 8, or 9 on each item.

Besides providing a measure that does not require your teachers to understand standard deviations at a sophisticated level, this approach has the advantage of focusing the faculty's (and administration's) attention on the extent of positive response to each item. An added benefit of this approach is that it conforms to the required self-scoring system used with the ISM Stability Markers. Your faculty culture score is itself one of the Stability Markers, and the approach recommended here is the same approach used in scoring that marker.

Overview

ISM encourages faculty leaders to consider Part A of the Faculty Culture Profile instrument a companion piece to the Student Experience Profile instrument. Both are derived from the SES findings and connect strongly to ISM's conclusions regarding student performance, student satisfaction, and student enthusiasm. That being the case, it is likely that enhancing your faculty's scores on the faculty instrument will eventually be reflected in similarly enhanced scores on the student instrument.

As a faculty leader, be conscious, as well, of the importance of ISM's Characteristics of Professional Excellence. This list of research-derived teacher characteristics provides you with a set of items useful in individual-teacher evaluation and professional development.

Note the Characteristics of Professional Excellence, unlike the two profiles, is not a survey instrument. It is, rather, designed for use by individual teachers and their administrative supervisors in designing professional development and evaluation-related targets that are simultaneously specific to each teacher and yet broadly related to ISM's findings in the Student Experience Study.

The ISM Faculty Culture Profile

This faculty culture instrument links strongly to the ISM findings in the Student Experience Study regarding student performance, student satisfaction, and student enthusiasm. Your own school's outcomes from the two instruments may profitably be considered companion pieces in your ongoing efforts to monitor the extent to which "predictability and support" conditions are present, and how strongly so, within your teaching and learning environment.

Part A: Faculty culture items related to the Student Experience Profile

Circle only one number for each item. Consider only the most recent grading period in your responses.

1. I and my colleagues find ways to make it obvious to all students that we wish them success every day, both in school and outside of school.

   1   2   3   4   5   6   7   8   9
   Not true of us at all   Exactly true of us

2. I and my colleagues find ways to make it obvious to all students that we want them to become better, more virtuous people (in ways consistent with our school's stated purposes and projected outcomes for our graduates).

   1   2   3   4   5   6   7   8   9
   Not true of us at all   Exactly true of us

3. I and my colleagues set clearly articulated standards for student academic performance.

| 1 | 2 | 3 | 4 | 5 | 6 | 7 | 8 | 9 |

Not true of us at all   Exactly true of us

4. I and my colleagues set reasonable, defensible standards for student behavior.

| 1 | 2 | 3 | 4 | 5 | 6 | 7 | 8 | 9 |

Not true of us at all   Exactly true of us

5. I and my colleagues are continually alert to the threat of unkind behavior between and among our students.

| 1 | 2 | 3 | 4 | 5 | 6 | 7 | 8 | 9 |

Not true of us at all   Exactly true of us

6. In confrontations with students, I and my colleagues conduct ourselves in ways that leave students' dignity intact regardless of the nature of the issue or infraction.

| 1 | 2 | 3 | 4 | 5 | 6 | 7 | 8 | 9 |

Not true of us at all   Exactly true of us

7. I and my colleagues individually and collectively demonstrate believably high levels of enthusiasm for teaching and learning and for the content of our studies.

| 1 | 2 | 3 | 4 | 5 | 6 | 7 | 8 | 9 |

Not true of us at all   Exactly true of us

8. I and my colleagues demonstrate through words and actions a genuine, believable commitment to the school, its purposes, its leadership, and each other.

| 1 | 2 | 3 | 4 | 5 | 6 | 7 | 8 | 9 |

Not true of us at all   Exactly true of us

9. I and my colleagues are glad to arrive at school and to see our students each day.

| 1 | 2 | 3 | 4 | 5 | 6 | 7 | 8 | 9 |

Not true of us at all   Exactly true of us

10. I and my colleagues create predictable tests (not to be confused either with "simple" tests or with "easy" assessments); our students can rely on the test preparation we offer them.

    1   2   3   4   5   6   7   8   9

Not true of us at all   Exactly true of us

11. I and my colleagues provide fair, reliable, understandable grade and reward structures for our students; our students are led to understand why they receive the grades they receive—high or low—and thereby to see how improvement, if they will seek it, be possible.

    1   2   3   4   5   6   7   8   9

Not true of us at all   Exactly true of us

12. I and my colleagues enforce our rules, justly, fairly, consistently.

    1   2   3   4   5   6   7   8   9

Not true of us at all   Exactly true of us

13. I and my colleagues are able to present ourselves each day in ways that will be seen by our students as consistent and reliable (i.e., unaffected by outside-of-school problems).

    1   2   3   4   5   6   7   8   9

Not true of us at all   Exactly true of us

Part B: Faculty culture items related to the original ISM study of students and teachers, and found in the Faculty Culture Profile I

14. I and my colleagues individually and collectively pursue career-long professional development as a foremost priority.

    1   2   3   4   5   6   7   8   9

Not true of us at all   Exactly true of us

15. I and my colleagues have mastered at least one pedagogical approach—not necessarily the same one for all of us—that is supported by reliable, contemporary research outcomes.

    1   2   3   4   5   6   7   8   9

Not true of us at all   Exactly true of us

16. When I and my colleagues are in casual conversations with each other, those conversations tend to be constructive, upbeat and professional.

    1   2   3   4   5   6   7   8   9

Not true of us at all   Exactly true of us

17. I and my colleagues have great respect for our division and school administrators.

    1   2   3   4   5   6   7   8   9

Not true of us at all   Exactly true of us

18. I and my colleagues find that our division and school administrators are highly supportive of our division's and school's faculty.

    1   2   3   4   5   6   7   8   9

Not true of us at all   Exactly true of us

19. I and my colleagues find that our division and school administrators are highly supportive of our division's and school's students.

    1   2   3   4   5   6   7   8   9

Not true of us at all   Exactly true of us

20. I and my colleagues find that our division and school administrators are highly supportive of our division's and school's parents.

    1   2   3   4   5   6   7   8   9

Not true of us at all   Exactly true of us

To score the Faculty Culture Profile using the method that will conform to appropriate self-scoring on the ISM Stability Marker pertaining to the quality of the faculty culture, use the following method. [Note 3] On any item on which 75% of the faculty members score at the top third of the response scale (i.e., 75% of the faculty circling the 7, 8, or 9), award one point. After determining the total (a number between 0 and 20), multiply that number by 0.3, thus converting the outcome to the six-point scale required by that item in the Stability Markers.

* The phrases "those in faculty leadership positions" or "faculty leaders" are used in reference to educators who may play a part in faculty- and student-culture enhancement, e.g., School Heads, Division Heads, Academic Deans, Academic Department Chairs, grade-level coordinators, Athletics Directors, or teachers serving on what ISM has termed Evaluation Design Teams

APPENDICES

The ISM Executive Leadership Study

Research and experience has led ISM to hypothesize that the School Head's well-being significantly relates to school outcomes. ISM conducted a study of School Heads to extend our knowledge of executive leadership and investigate the relationship among School Heads' characteristics and experience, and their well-being.

Great leaders can transform a school and take it to new heights, whereas poor leaders can cause great challenges for schools. We have long asserted that, as the executive leader, your "style" does not seem to account for the differences in organizational performance. Nonetheless, you are a critical component of a school's ability to deliver its mission with excellence. If it is not style, then what are the critical aspects of executive leaders that separate the best leaders from the rest?

Our existing measure of executive leadership comprises ISM's Stability Marker No. 3. It is a 20-item measure rating School Head leadership traits and points of emphasis, as perceived by the faculty, that translate into the Head's ability to foster a healthy faculty culture. The measure is commensurate with our model, ISM X. (See Chapter 5.) In ISM X, "Executive Leadership" occupies a critical point at which the strategic plan and strategic financial plan, with the school's resources, is translated into a healthy school culture. Such a culture maximizes student performance, enthusiasm, and satisfaction through the faculty, providing a predictable and supportive environment driven by a common commitment to professional growth and renewal within a professional learning community. These factors in turn produce enrollment demand and are related to the long-term viability of the school.

Our existing research into executive leadership found the following ideas and concepts are essential to producing a strong faculty culture. A strong School Head is:

- *charismatic*: as evidenced by an on-campus public presence that is seen as gracious, respectful, contemplative, self-effacing, and humble, yet at the same time infused with a sense of moral purpose and integrity perceived by all as nonnegotiable and impervious to political pressure;
- *flexible*: willing to engage in "conversation" with others while moving toward a decision and being open to being influenced by that conversation;
- *predictable*: consistently responds to events, both "good" and "bad";
- *supportive*: discriminately provides support when merited; and,
- *an effective communicator*: gracious, respectful, fluent and articulate in public communication forums, written and oral.

The goal of leadership is to optimize an organization's performance. To achieve this for a school, the Head must attend to the "process" (strategy, goals, and actions) and people (listening, inspiring, changing beliefs, gaining commitment, crafting culture). We have observed that the performance of people is inextricably tied to their well-being and that of their leaders. Thus, we wondered if the School Head's well-being should be added to this list of essential characteristics that drive outcomes in private schools. Studies in the public sector on the impact and importance of the School Principal support this notion.

- In 2007, the National Staff Development Council identified the three strands of school leadership as including academic focus, shared beliefs and values, and productive professional relationships. The report highlighted a caring and personal climate, trust, as well as honest and open communications.
- In 2009, a Wallace Foundation report indicated that, after teacher quality,

school leadership was the second most important influence on student learning.

- In 2008, Calder Urban Institute published "Estimating Principal Effectiveness," which suggested that Principals who stayed in a school longer were more effective. Yet, in 2014, the National Center for Education Statistics reported in "Principal Attrition and Mobility" (including private schools) that 20% of private School Heads turn over each year. Many leave education entirely.
- In 2013, a National Association of Elementary School Principals summary of Principal leadership research identified isolation and a workload that seems insurmountable as two of four reasons Principals left the position.

Study Description and Summary Statistics

In 2016, we invited Heads and their faculties to complete a survey that examined their well-being and the stability of their schools. Stability was defined by the first Tier of Stability Markers, including:

– cash reserves, debt, and endowment;

– the existence of a strategic plan and strategic financial plan;

– executive leadership (measured through a faculty questionnaire);

– hard-income coverage;

– faculty culture (measured through a faculty questionnaire); and

– enrollment demand in excess of supply.

Well-being was determined by two measures, including the Diener Flourishing Scale and the Diener Subjective Well-being Scale (Life Satisfaction). Participants answered questions about their experience of trust, predictability, and support apparent between the Head and the Board and the Head and his or her direct reports. Given that "being an effective communicator," particularly in public and group situations, is a key competency noted in our existing measure of executive leadership, a brief measure of social facility was given to assess the School Head's confidence in social and public speaking situations.

Following two rounds (spring and fall) of participation requests:

– 210 School Heads began the set of survey instruments;

– 131 School Heads completed the set of items, with an average length of time in education of 25.06 years;

– 90 Heads reported being in their first headship; and

– the mean length of time in their current position was 7.5 years, while the median length was five years, indicating that a few longer-term Heads skewed the arithmetic mean upward. The set of schools that comprised the 131 participants was not significantly dissimilar to other data sets we have collected, suggesting a representative sample despite the voluntary nature of the data collection.

Because Stability Marker No. 3 (Executive Leadership) and No. 5 (Faculty Culture) are necessarily completed by the schools' teachers, School Heads emailed a link to their faculties inviting them to complete these confidential measures. While teachers from 89 schools began the survey, 40 schools had both complete School Head data and sufficient faculty response to the measures. There were no significant variations in the summary statistics or the correlation matrix among the School-Head-completed variables in the two sample sets (131 vs. 40).

Results Summary

Multiple regression was the primary method of statistical analysis for this study. Significant bivariate correlations lead us to conclude, as expected, that executive leadership is significantly related to school performance and culture. Further, the well-being of executive leaders matters, and is significantly related to the leader's ability to produce a strong faculty culture and key school outcomes. Specifically, we found significant correlations among the following.

- Executive Leadership (Stability Marker No. 3) and
  - Enrollment Demand ($r = 0.31$);
  - Faculty Culture ($r = 0.51$); and;
  - Predictability and Support with the Board ($r = 0.32$).
- Head's Flourishing (Well-being) and
  - School Stability (Sum of Tier 1 Stability Markers) ($r = 0.46$);
  - Faculty Culture ($r = 0.41$);
  - Trust (with Board and Direct Reports) ($r = 0.52$);
  - Predictability and Support with the Board ($r = 0.42$); and
  - Current Tenure as Head ($r = 0.39$).
- Current Tenure and Stability Marker No. 1 (Debt, Cash Reserves, Endowment Mix) ($r = 0.34$).

Of note is that, while the length of time in their position was correlated to the school's financial stability, experience in education and as a Head was not correlated with any other variables including school performance, faculty culture, and the School Head's well-being. Leadership matters and tenure are related to school stability. Experience, however, appears unrelated to school performance and the well-being of the Head.

As with any correlation, causal direction cannot be determined, but we are equally comfortable asserting that well-being influences the Head's success, your faculty's culture, and your school's performance—including enrollment demand. At the same time, your school's performance, the support you experience, and the faculty culture influence your well-being. Again, while subsequent studies will provide deeper analysis of the data and more specific recommendations, in general, you should not allow the demands of the Head's stressful position to cause you to cast aside the healthy behaviors that mitigate that stress. Instead, the Head should make his or her own social-emotional well-being a top priority.

From our research, ISM has determined two primary strategic outcome variables for independent schools are:

- financial stability (Stability Marker No. 1), which ISM defines as the positive mix of cash reserves, low debt, and endowment; and
- enrollment demand (Stability Marker No. 6), which ISM defines as 90%+ retention and full-class waiting pools at entry grades.

Related to Stability Marker No. 1, there was only one positive significant factor: length of tenure of the School Head. No other variables were retained. This finding may be obvious—School Heads who encounter financial trouble are more likely to be let go by their Boards. However, we speculate that, while true, it is more complex than that. Success on Stability Marker No. 1 does not just rest on the quality of the executive leader. It is highly dependent on a high-functioning strategic Board that approves budgets aimed to achieve financial stability (i.e., 20% cash reserve, annual debt service < 5% of expenses, etc.).

Perhaps more important, success on Stability Marker No. 1 most likely occurs when a Board creates a predictable and supportive environment within which the Head can serve productively. A high-quality, supportive Board gives the Head time to formulate and execute a school improvement plan, move the wrong people "off the bus" and the right people "on the bus" and in the "right seats," improve the school culture, realign the school mission with school practice and brand identity, etc. This all moves a school toward sustainable annual surpluses that can accelerate debt reduction and a build-up of rainy-day money. We have argued in the past that School Heads need longer tenure than the current average.

One of the many reasons why Heads leave their schools is because their relationships with their Boards are not as supportive or trusting as they must be. One of the major themes throughout this discussion is that the Head's perception of the Board-Head relationship is a significant factor in school outcomes. The relationship between the financial stability of a school and the length of Head tenure is also likely dependent on the presence of an environment in which the Head wants to stay long term.

Enrollment demand was best predicted by three factors, represented by the following equation. These three factors accounted for 30% of the variance in enrollment demand.

$$\textbf{Enrollment Demand} = \text{strategic plan and strategic financial plan} + \text{Executive Leadership} - \text{Social Facility.}$$
$$R = .55, R^2 = .30, p < .01$$

The first factor is the presence of a formal strategic plan and an accompanying strategic financial plan (Stability Marker No. 2). The second factor is our measure of executive leadership. This is a 20-item inventory, completed by faculty, which measures the characteristics of leadership and points of emphasis of the School Head that are associated with building a strong faculty culture. Having a plan and being a strong leader is associated with greater enrollment demand.

Social facility or extraversion was measured in the study since effective communication is identified by ISM as an essential characteristic of a school leader. It is noteworthy that social facility was significant, but with a negative coefficient. School Heads, it seems, must be confident and comfortable, but not overly bold, aggressive, or grandiose in their communication. They must solicit input from others and relate a clear, strategic focus to others. This finding supports ISM's previous studies on executive leadership, suggesting that while leadership style does not matter, the level of charisma—as marked by having a gracious, respectful, contemplative, self-effacing, and humble presence—does matter.

ISM asserts that enrollment demand is impacted through the Board's creation of a quadrennial strategic plan with an accompanying strategic financial plan. Tactically, this plan is translated by executive leadership into a healthy school culture that needs to be effectively, internally marketed. Our School Head study has confirmed this teaching. The result, noted above, of an inverse relationship between the scores on Stability Marker No. 1 and the presence of a plan suggests that schools tend to only employ such a plan when their financial picture is weak. This should stand as a keen warning to all schools. If schools want long-term stability, then a strategic plan and strategic financial plan are essential. Waiting to construct a formal plan until the school is in financial peril is to place your enrollment demand in jeopardy.

The Head Leadership Study explains that the quality of the executive leader (aka, the School Head) as perceived by the faculty is correlated with enrollment demand. Leaders who are charismatic, flexible, predictable, supportive, effective communicators, and not overly extraverted appear to produce greater enrollment demand. We note the Board's role in enrollment demand through the strategic plan and strategic financial plan and, thus, the Board-Head strategic relationship is also correlated with enrollment demand. Finally, we suggest that overly extraverted Heads often negatively impact enrollment demand and should exercise discretion in their communication. This connection of enrollment demand to the School Head is a real leap forward in our understanding of the factors that impact a family's willingness to enroll and re-enroll.

The Faculty Experience Survey

Consider in your responses only the three most recent months unless otherwise instructed. Score each statement on a 1 to 9 scale with "1" being "not true at all" and "9" being "exactly true." The focus in this survey is on the overall climate of the school; the focus is not on the individual. Each question begins with the phrase, "I and my colleagues." Although you cannot speak with complete accuracy for your colleagues, for the purpose of this survey, please provide your perspective as well as your impressions of your colleagues' perspectives on the issues.

   1   2   3   4   5   6   7   8   9

Not true of us at all   *Exactly true of us*

I and my colleagues

1. understand exactly how we are evaluated.
2. view our evaluation procedures as consistent (i.e., predictable).
3. view our evaluation procedures as constructive (i.e., helpful).
4. view our faculty culture as appropriately supportive (as evidenced by collegial interaction).

5. view our school's administrative culture (i.e., the collective attitude of all our administrative staff members, including those in the Business Office, Development Office, Admission Office, and so on) as appropriately supportive of the faculty: i.e., wishing our success and striving to support us in our efforts.
6. find the administrator(s) who supervises and/or evaluates us is highly supportive of us: i.e., hopes for our success and is focused on our growth and renewal as professionals.
7. agree the administrator(s) who supervises and/or evaluates us provides us with accurate reinforcement regarding our performance as faculty members.
8. agree the administrator(s) who supervises and/or evaluates us demonstrates consistent responses on a daily basis, i.e., we find that we know what to expect from her or him in all situations.
9. agree the administrator(s) who supervises us and/or evaluates us provides clarity of expectations.
10. agree the administrator(s) who supervises us and/or evaluates us is eager to assist us in meeting those expectations.

Scoring

A. Average the mean scores for items 3, 4, 5, 6, and 10 to obtain the supportiveness score.

B. Average the mean scores for items 1, 2, 7, 8, and 9 to obtain the predictability score.

C. Go to the ISM Faculty Experience Matrix (Figure 10.1) and use the cutoff scores along the corresponding axis to plot the school's current quadrant.

www.ingramcontent.com/pod-product-compliance
Lightning Source LLC
Chambersburg PA
CBHW082059230426
43670CB00017B/2894